♥ LOGO DESIGN LOVE

a guide to creating iconic brand identities

from david airey

New Riders | VOICES THAT MATTER™

Logo Design Love: A Guide to Creating Iconic Brand Identities

David Airey

New Riders
1249 Eighth Street
Berkeley, CA 94710
510/524-2178
510/524-2221 (fax)

Find us on the Web at: www.newriders.com
To report errors, please send a note to errata@peachpit.com

New Riders is an imprint of Peachpit, a division of Pearson Education

Acquisitions editor: Nikki Echler McDonald
Development editors: Robin Drake and Jill Marts Lodwig
Production editor: Cory Borman
Indexer: Jack Lewis
Cover and interior design: David Airey

ISBN 13   978-0-321-66076-3
ISBN 10   0-321-66076-5

9 8 7 6 5

Printed and bound in the United States of America

About the author

David Airey, a graphic designer from Northern Ireland, has been intrigued by brand identity since the 1990s, when he enrolled in his first graphic design course. Having honed his skills working in the United Kingdom and the United States, he then made a conscious choice to specialize in brand identity design, where his passion lies.

Self-employed since 2005, David has amassed an impressive global client list, including the likes of Yellow Pages™ (Canada), Giacom (England), and Berthier Associates (Japan).

He writes two of the most popular graphic design blogs on the Internet, logodesignlove.com and davidairey.com, attracting more than 250,000 online visitors per month and approximately 1 million monthly page views.

Contributors (a huge thanks)

160over90	160over90.com
300million	300million.com
Andrew Sabatier	andrewsabatier.com
biz-R	biz-r.co.uk
Bunch	bunchdesign.com
Fertig Design	fertigdesign.com
Gerard Huerta	gerardhuerta.com
id29	id29.com
Ivan Chermayeff	cgstudionyc.com
Jerry Kuyper	jerrykuyper.com
Jonathan Selikoff	selikoffco.com
Josiah Jost	siahdesign.com
Kevin Burr	ocularink.com
Landor	landor.com
Lindon Leader	leadercreative.com
Logo Motive Designs	logomotive.net
Maggie Macnab	macnabdesign.com
Malcolm Grear Designers	mgrear.com
Michael Kosmicki	hellosubsist.com
Mike Rohde	rohdesign.com
Moon Brand	moonbrand.com
Muamer Adilovic	muameradilovic.com
Nancy Wu	nancywudesign.com
nido	thisisnido.com
Roy Smith	roysmithdesign.com
Rudd Studio	ruddstudio.com
smashLAB	smashlab.com
SomeOne	someoneinlondon.com
Stephen Lee Ogden	stephenleeogden.com
studio1500	studio1500sf.com
UnderConsideration	underconsideration.com

Contents

Introduction   x

I   The importance of brand identity

Chapter one   **No escape!**   2

Chapter two   **It's the stories we tell**   8
None genuine without this signature   9
A logoless company is a faceless man   10
Seen by millions   11
Only if the Queen agrees   12
Symbols transcend boundaries   13
Identity design as part of our language   18
Rethinking the importance of brand identity   21

Chapter three   **Elements of iconic design**   22
Keep it simple   22
Make it relevant   25
Incorporate tradition   28
Aim for distinction   30
Commit to memory   33
Think small   34
Focus on one thing   36
The seven ingredients in your signature dish   38
Remember that rules are made to be broken   39

II   The process of design

Chapter four   **Laying the groundwork**   42
Shaking out the jitters   42
It's all in the design brief   43
Gathering preliminary information   44
Asking the tougher questions   45
Give your client time and space   48

	But maintain the focus	48
	Homework time	48
	Assembling the design brief	49
	A mission and some objectives hold the key	50
	Field research to the rescue	53
	Bringing the details of client discussions to life	56
	Culling the adjectives supplied by the client	59
Chapter five	**Skirting the hazards of a redesign**	**62**
	What are the reasons for rebranding?	63
	Don't squeeze too hard	63
	When emotions run high	67
	Answers often lie in focus groups	68
	From "unresponsive" to "caring"	69
	Maybe just some tweaking?	72
	Remember your manners	75
Chapter six	**Pricing design**	**76**
	The design pricing formula	76
	Hourly rates or a set fee?	81
	Handling print costs	82
	Receipt of a down payment	84
	The money exchange	85
	Spec work	87
	Everyone makes mistakes	89
Chapter seven	**From pencil to PDF**	**90**
	Mind-mapping	90
	The fundamental necessity of the sketchpad	96
	The Tenth Commandment	98
	Pinning the map	102
	Internationally recognized	104
	No set time	107
	Dress for success	109
	Black and white before color	111
	Where Photoshop comes into play	114
	The pen is mightier than the mouse	116

Chapter eight	**The art of the conversation**	**118**
	Deal with the decision-maker	119
	Rule #1: Conspire to help	124
	Rule #2: Avoid intermediation	126
	Rule #3: Take control	128
	Rule #4: Keep the committee involved	132
	Don't forget to under-promise and then over-deliver	134
	Swallow that pride	136

III   **Keep the fires burning**

Chapter nine	**Staying motivated**	**144**
	Never stop learning	145
	Be four years ahead	147
	Create for you	148
	Step away from the computer	149
	Balance your life	150
	Journey back in time	150
	Show relentless desire	151
	But don't overwork yourself	151
	We all get stuck, no matter who we are	152
	Start on the right foot, and stay on the right foot	153
	Find common ground	153
	Deadline looming	154
	Think laterally	155
	Improve how you communicate	156
	Manage your expectations	156
	Always design	157
	Follow your bliss	157
	Not everyone is as fortunate	159

Chapter ten	**Your questions answered**	**160**
	Similar looking logos	160
	Rights of use	161

Online portfolio creation	162
Seal the deal	167
Overseas clients	168
How many concepts?	169
Friends and family	170
Design revisions	171
Project time frames	172
Researching the competition	173
Internships	173
Worst client project	174
Tools of the trade	175
Handling the workload	176
Who owns what?	177

Chapter eleven

25 practical logo design tips	**178**
1. Questions, questions, questions	178
2. Understand print costs	179
3. Expect the unexpected	179
4. A logo doesn't need to say what a company does	180
5. Not every logo needs a mark	180
6. One thing to remember	181
7. Don't neglect the sketchpad	182
8. Leave trends to the fashion industry	183
9 Step away from Photoshop	183
10. Work in black and white	184
11. Keep it relevant	184
12. Remember legibility	185
13. Be consistent	185
14. Match the type to the mark	186
15. Offer a single-color version	186
16. Pay attention to contrast	187
17. Aid recognition	187
18. Test at a variety of sizes	187
19. Reverse it	188
20. Turn it upside down	188
21. Consider trademarking your design	189

22. Don't neglect the substrate   190
23. Don't be afraid of mistakes   190
24. A logo is not a brand   190
25. Remember, it's a two-way process   191

Design resources   **Help from elsewhere**   **192**
                        Graphic design blogs   192
                        Iconic designers   193
                        Recommended books   194

Index   **Looking for something?**   **198**

Introduction

Brand identity design. Who needs it? Every company on the planet. Who provides the service? You.

But how do you win big-name clients? And how do you stay relevant? Design is an ever-evolving profession. If you're like me, one of your goals as a graphic designer is to always improve your skills so that you can attract the clients you want. So it's vital that you keep learning and growing.

This book is about sharing with you everything that I know about creating brand identities so that you can stay motivated and inspired, and make smart and well-informed decisions when procuring and working with your clients.

But who am I, and what reason do you have for heeding my advice?

Well, for a number of years I've been sharing design projects on my blogs at davidairey.com and logodesignlove.com. In these blogs, I walk my readers through the individual stages of my identity design projects. I talk about how I sealed the deal with a client. I examine the details of a design brief. And I describe how a client might sign off on polished artwork.

My websites currently generate 1 million monthly page views and have a combined subscriber count of more than 30,000 readers. That's quite a lot for a young lad from Bangor, Northern Ireland. My readers tell me that reading my blogs makes them feel like they're getting to go "behind the scenes" into my design process, and that it's difficult to find such insights elsewhere. They say that my features are helpful, inspiring, and very much appreciated (and I didn't pay them for their comments, I promise!).

If you search through the portfolios of the most successful design agencies and studios, you'll find plenty of examples of final design work. Some portfolios might even show one or two alternative concepts. For the most part, however, we can find very little of what actually happens between designers and their clients: the questions they ask to get projects started on the right foot, how they generate ideas after creating and studying the design brief, and how they present their designs to win their client's approval. Such details are like gold dust to a designer.

And so, the idea for this book was born.

Never before have I gone into so much detail about my design process, and never before have I studied the intricacies in such depth. In the process, I've brought many talented designers and design studios on board who very graciously have shared their own thoughts, processes, and advice.

When you finish reading this book, you hopefully will be well-prepared to go out and win your own clients and create your own iconic brand identities. Had I known about everything contained in this book when I first started my own graphic design business, I would definitely have saved myself a lot of worrying and restless nights.

Part I

The importance of brand identity

Chapter one
No escape! (33 logos in 33 minutes)

Logos bombard us. Think clothes labels, running shoes, TVs, and computers. From the moment we wake to the moment we sleep, they're an ever-present part of our daily routine.

07:01

The average American sees 16,000 advertisements, logos, and labels in a day, said Dharma Singh Khalsa, M.D., in his book *Brain Longevity*.[1]

Don't believe it?

To illustrate the constant presence of logos in our lives, I decided to spend the first few minutes of a typical working day photographing logos on the products I interact with, beginning with my morning alarm.

The following sequence tells a story of its own, providing a brief glimpse into my daily routine, which is not to say that there weren't plenty of other logos around me at the time— on other food products, books and newspapers, TV shows, and my clothing.

[1] Dharma Singh Khalsa, M.D. with Cameron Stauth. *Brain Longevity: The Breakthrough Medical Program That Improves Your Mind and Memory*. (New York, NY: Grand Central Publishing, 1999).

07:02

07:03

07:04

07:05

07:06

07:07

07:08

07:09

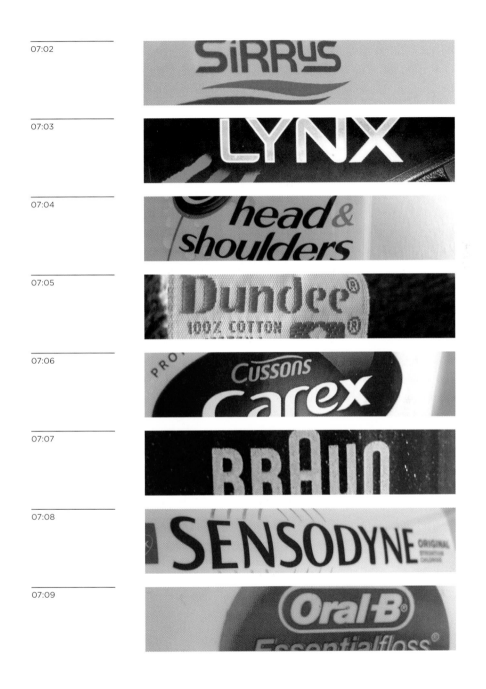

07:10

07:11

07:12

07:13

07:14

07:15

07:16

07:17

07:18

07:19

07:20

07:21

07:22

07:23

07:24

07:25

07:26

07:27

07:28

07:29

07:30

07:31

07:32

07:33

Try it yourself. Maybe not as soon as you wake up. But what about right at this moment? Look around. How many logos can you see?

Reuters magazine proclaimed in 1997 that "In the last 30 years, mankind has produced more information than in the previous 5,000."[2] Because humanity is now producing such a vast amount of information, we're seeing logos that are increasingly similar to one another. This poses a problem for companies that are trying to differentiate themselves visually, but it also creates an opportunity for designers who are skilled enough to create iconic designs that stand above the crowd.

The Guild of Food Writers

By 300million

2005

Take, for instance, 300million, one of the United Kingdom's top creative agencies, which spent two weeks creating and crafting this logo, making excellent use of negative space to show a spoon inside a pen nib.

"What you take away is just as important as what you keep," said Katie Morgan, senior designer at 300million.

Seeing just one great design like this is a testament to the work of creative agencies like 300million, as well as ideal inspiration for designers everywhere who continually strive to create brilliant designs. Let's take a look at a few more in Chapter 2.

[2]   "Information Overload Causes Stress." *Reuters* magazine, March/April 1997. Lexis/Nexis Academic Universe. London: Reuters Group PLC.

Chapter two
It's the stories we tell

Why is branding important? Because people often choose products based on their perceived value rather than their actual value.

Think about the celebrity who drives an Aston Martin instead of, say, a Skoda, which is continually ranked "car of the year" in many European countries and delivers much better mileage at a significantly cheaper price. Sure, Skoda is the logical choice, but it's Aston Martin's identity, which conjures images of luxury and status, that usually clinches the sale. Then there's Lexus versus Scion. Which would most people pay more for, and why?

Scion

By Fresh Machine

2002

Lexus

By Molly Designs

Refined by Siegel+Gale

2002

With the right branding, businesses can increase their product's perceived value, establish relationships with their customers that span ages and borders, and nurture those relationships into a lifelong bond.

Of course, it always helps to have a good story to tell. Your job as a designer is to find the story, and tell it wisely. The rest of this chapter shares a few examples of designers who got it just right.

None genuine without this signature

Will Keith (W.K.) Kellogg invented wheat flakes and then corn flakes, spawning a breakfast cereal revolution and helping to develop an industry that has since become one of the most successful on the planet. But we might never have been familiar with the Kellogg name if W.K. hadn't also been such a smart business strategist.

Kellogg developed marketing campaigns that were years ahead of their time. He used modern, four-color print advertising in magazines and on billboards at a time when other companies were still thinking in black and white. And to distinguish Kellogg's Corn Flakes from those manufactured by other cereal companies, he made sure all of his boxes bore the legend, "Beware of Imitations. None Genuine Without This Signature, W.K. Kellogg."

Kellogg's signature

By W.K. Kellogg

1906

Kellogg still uses the same trademark signature that it has been using since 1906 on the front of every pack of cereal, but these days the signature is a red, stylized version. This consistency built a level of trust and repeat business with consumers through the years, which has helped establish Kellogg as the world's leading cereal manufacturer.

A logoless company is a faceless man

For thousands of years, humans have needed and desired social identification. Think of the farmer who brands his cattle to mark his ownership, or the stonemason who proudly chisels his trademark.

When you close your eyes and picture McDonald's, what do you see? Golden arches, perhaps? For those products and services that have a strong brand identity, it's the identity that people often think of first, rather than the product itself. Think of Microsoft, Apple, Ford, and Target. Chances are good that without even showing you the logos, you'd have a fairly good picture of how they look. Granted, a huge marketing budget is necessary to achieve the recognition rates of such organizations, but it's important to "put on your best face."

By Gerard Huerta

Type Directors
Club

1994

TIME magazine

1977

Waldenbooks

1979

Iconic designer Gerard Huerta, born and raised in Southern California, has been producing well-known identities for decades, including those for the likes of *TIME*, Waldenbooks, and the Type Directors Club. You are probably just as familiar, if not more familiar, with these logos as you are with the products or services themselves.

Seen by millions

By summer 2008, J.K. Rowling's *Harry Potter* book series had sold more than 400 million copies and was translated into 67 languages. So when New York design and creative firm id29 was chosen in 2007 to create the campaign and associated identity elements for the seventh book, it was clear that its work would be seen by millions (or even billions).

Harry Potter 7

By id29

Designer and art director: Doug Bartow

Creative director: Michael Fallone

2007

Seen in Times Square, New York

"We came up with a distinctive campaign aesthetic based on a central typographic element that we could use across all different media, from printed posters and bookmarks to rich media and online applications," said Doug Bartow, design director and principal at id29.

Makes sense. Think about the traffic passing through Times Square. Most people don't have time to be reading from billboards, so a symbol is much more fitting. Using a simple mark to identify the campaign allowed those taking even the briefest of glimpses to recognize news of the book release.

"The results were phenomenal, with *Harry Potter and the Deathly Hallows* selling 8.3 million copies in the United States within the first 24 hours of its release," said Bartow.

Only if the Queen agrees

The Queen of England—head of state and head of a nation—understands the importance of brand identity.

Moon Brand, a branding and communications consultancy based in London, needed final approval from Her Majesty on this design for the Royal Parks.

The Royal Parks

By Moon Brand

Designers:
Richard Moon,
Ceri Webber,
Andy Locke

2006

THE
ROYAL
PARKS

"The leaves we chose to use in this logo are from indigenous British trees found in the Royal Parks," said Moon Brand director Richard Moon.

The logo tells the story of the parks using their own language—leaves—and deftly portrays the relationship between the park system and the British crown with one clever picture. This clarity helped the project through to completion.

Moon Brand was told that approval from the Queen can take months, but it came back within 24 hours.

Symbols transcend boundaries

To sell products internationally, your brand has to speak a lot of different languages. Fortunately, easy-to-identify symbols need no translation. Recognizable regardless of culture or language, symbols enable companies to cross language barriers, compete globally, and maintain brand consistency across a wide range of media.

Take, for example, international branding and design agency Bunch. Its designers used a seven-pointed star inspired by the Star of Bethlehem to brand a new two-story club, Star of Bethnal Green (SoBG), which opened in the heart of Bethnal Green in London in 2008. The hard-working star symbol, which is a play on the name of the club and its owner, Rob Star, was used on everything from note cards to pint glasses.

The symbol had to be a star in some guise, said Bunch Creative Director Denis Kovac, so the design team began playing around with the traditional five-pointed star. All too soon they realized that it was too commonplace.

**Star of
Bethnal Green
experimentation**

"We figured a five-pointed star would always be reminiscent of national flags, communism, and pagan rituals," said Kovac. "Rob Star already had a large following through his Mulletover club night, which brought to mind the expression 'follow the star.' He wanted the pub to be a shining beacon in Bethnal Green, attracting people from far and wide. The Star of Bethlehem with seven points and a long tail presented itself as a way forward."

**Star of
Bethnal Green
sketches**

While Kovac and his team produced many possible variations, it was a simple thick-outlined star that was chosen, not only because it was a brilliant design, but also because it could be used as a template and altered to suit any application or theme.

**The Star of
Bethnal Green**

By Bunch

2008

Bunch used the versatile star symbol on bottles, food, DJ paraphernalia, and stationery. Inside the pub, pint glasses are etched with the simplest form of the star, and screen-printed wallpaper features the same design drawn by hand.

Bunch's project is a classic lesson in versatility. When designing brand identity, you must always ask yourself whether your logo can adapt to different media.

**Pint glasses and
business cards**

Identity design as part of our language

biz-R, a design studio in England, created this logotype with its customized typeface for Amanda Marsden, a lifestyle salon and spa based in Devon, England. The designers then extrapolated the letters "am" from the design, which represent the client's initials and form the word "am," to create a contemporary minimalist wordmark.

Amanda Marsden

By biz-R

2008

amanda marsden

The word was then integrated into the various phrases used to promote Marsden's service, such as "am: beautiful," "am: relaxed," and the "am: gifted" card (shown opposite).

Not every brand name will suit such a language-centric approach, but keep it in mind, because it's one more tool in your design arsenal that you can employ when the time is right.

Rethinking the importance of brand identity

We often do judge books by their covers, whether it's fair or not. And that's why the perceived value of a service or product is usually greater than the actual one. The same visual identity seen time and again builds trust, and trust keeps customers coming back for more. It's kind of like putting a face to a name— logos help people remember their experiences with companies.

You might practice making these very important points during initial discussions with your clients, as a way of driving home the importance of choosing you as their designer.

Chapter three

Elements of iconic design

Anyone can design a logo, but not everyone can design the right logo. A successful design may meet the goals set in your design brief, but a truly enviable iconic design will also be simple, relevant, enduring, distinctive, memorable, and adaptable.

So many requirements may seem like a tall order, and it is. But remember, you have to know the rules in any creative endeavor before you can successfully break them. A Michelin-star chef doesn't just pluck ingredients from thin air. She takes a tried-and-tested recipe and adapts it to create her signature dish. This also applies to creating brand identities. The basic elements of classic iconic brand identities are the ingredients in our recipe, so let's examine each one closely before you go out and earn your own awards.

Keep it simple

The simplest solution is often the most effective. Why? Because a simple logo helps meet most of the other requirements of iconic design.

Simplicity helps a design be more versatile. Adopting a minimalist approach enables your logo to be used across a wide range of media, such as on business cards, billboards, pin badges, or even a small website favicon.

Simplicity also makes your design easier to recognize, so it stands a greater chance of achieving a timeless, enduring quality. Think of the logos of large corporations like Mitsubishi, Samsung, FedEx, BBC, and so on. Their logos are simple, and they're easier to recognize because of it.

FedEx

By Lindon Leader

1994

And simplicity helps people remember your design. Consider how our minds work, and how it's much easier to remember a single detail, such as Mona Lisa's smile, than it is to remember five: the clothes Mona Lisa wears, how her hands are placed, the colour of her eyes, what sits behind her, the artist (Leonardo da Vinci—but that one you did know, didn't you?). Look at it this way: If someone asked you to sketch the McDonald's logo, and then sketch the Mona Lisa, which would be more accurate?

Let's look at a different example.

The National Health Service (NHS) logo is one of the most visible logos in the United Kingdom, so much so that its use as the emblem of British health care was made government policy in 2000.

National Health Service (NHS)

By Moon Brand

Designer:
Richard Moon

1990

Initially designed in 1990 by Moon Brand, this logo includes a simple, clean color palette and type treatment. The fact that the design has remained unchanged for nearly 20 years is a testament to its success.

"We kept the design deliberately simple for three reasons: to make it easy to implement, to last as long as possible, and to go undetected by the British media who often see such identity programs as an extravagant use of public funds," said Richard Moon, director at Moon Brand. "By the NHS' own reckoning, the branding program has saved tens of millions in pounds by employing this distinctive, easy-to-use brand program."

Make it relevant

Any logo you design must be appropriate for the business it identifies. Are you designing for a lawyer? Then you need to ditch the fun approach. Are you designing for a winter-holiday TV program? No beach balls please. How about a cancer organization? A smiley face clearly won't work. I could go on, but you get the picture.

Your design must be relevant to the industry, your client, and the audience to which you're catering. Getting up to speed on all these aspects requires a lot of indepth research, but the investment of time is worth it: Without a strong knowledge of your client's world, you can't hope to create a design that successfully differentiates your client's business from its closest competitors.

Hawaiian Airlines

By Lindon Leader

1993

Keep in mind, though, that a logo doesn't have to go so far as to literally reveal what a company does. Think about the BMW logo, for instance. It isn't a car. And the Hawaiian Airlines logo isn't an airplane. But both stand out from the competition and are relevant within their respective worlds.

Josiah Jost of Siah Design, based in Alberta, Canada, worked with Ed's Electric, a local electrical company, to create a new brand identity. Not only did Josiah deliver a logo that is relevant, but he also created one that most viewers won't easily forget.

Ed's Electric

By Josiah Jost

2008

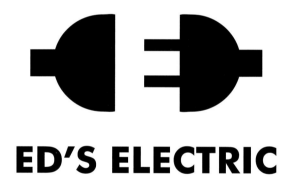

ED'S ELECTRIC

"With Ed's Electric, the logo idea popped into my head while I was trying to see something in the negative space in electrical elements," said Jost. "I knew right away that the concept was a winner."

Another Moon Brand design, this time for Vision Capital, epitomizes this notion of relevance as it pertains to brand identity. During extensive discussions with the client prior to commencing any creative work, Moon Brand designers discovered that Vision Capital is about more than just capital: It's also about raising funds for investors using a very strategic approach to buying company portfolios. So they decided to base their exploration on this "more than" idea.

Vision Capital

By Moon Brand

Designer:
Richard Moon

1990

The resulting logo conveys the concept in a clever way. By rotating the "V" for vision, it becomes the "greater than" symbol, allowing viewers to easily interpret the logo as signifying "greater (or more) than capital," while still clearly featuring the initials of the company.

Just because you're designing a logo that must relate to the stereotypically dull financial markets doesn't mean it can't be dynamic and full of meaning.

Incorporate tradition

When it comes to logo design and brand identity, it's best to leave trends to the fashion industry. Trends come and go like the wind and the last thing you want to do is invest a significant amount of your time and your client's money in a design that will become dated almost overnight. Longevity is key, and a logo should last for the duration of the business it represents. It might get refined after some time to add a little freshness, but the underlying idea should remain intact.

Vanderbilt University

By Malcolm Grear Designers

2002

VANDERBILT
UNIVERSITY

The Rhode-Island-based agency Malcolm Grear Designers created the visual identity for Vanderbilt by integrating two symbols long associated with the university: the oak leaf (strength and steadfastness) and the acorn (seed of knowledge). These elements also reflect the school's status as an active arboretum.

"The toughest person to please in any logo design project should be the designer who creates the mark," said Malcolm Grear. "It's challenging because the work must be memorable, as timeless as possible. I never want to be in vogue. I want to set the standard and not follow others."

Vanderbilt University

By Malcolm Grear Designers

2002

Aim for distinction

A distinctive logo is one that can be easily separated from the competition. It has a unique quality or style that accurately portrays your client's business perspective. But how do you create a logo that's unique?

The best strategy is to focus initially on a design that is recognizable. So recognizable, in fact, that just its shape or outline gives it away. Working in only black and white can help you create more distinctive marks, since the contrast emphasizes the shape or idea. Color really is secondary to the shape and form of your design.

NMA

By SomeOne

Design and
creative direction:
David Law

2003

SomeOne, a London-based design agency specializing in the launch and relaunch of brands, worked with the Newspaper Marketing Agency (NMA) to create two distinctive logos. The first, a monogram using the characters NMA, looks like it was fairly simple to create: mainly just a series of three sets of up and down strokes. Okay, so there's a little more to it—just coming up with the idea is the challenge—but the mark is bold, simple, and relevant. Most of all, it's distinctive and likely something viewers won't forget.

ANNAs

By SomeOne

Design and
creative direction:
David Law

2006

AWARDS for NATIONAL
NEWSPAPER ADVERTISING

The second logo is a stylish
"open newspaper" symbol
in the shape of the letter *A*
for the Awards for National
Newspaper Advertising (or
ANNAs). It works very well in
black and white. Notice how
easy it was for me to describe
it? That's because distinctive
marks are almost always simple
enough that they can be easily
described.

In another example, England-based designer nido cleverly
transforms the familiar letters *a* and *e* in "Talkmore," a
wholesaler of mobile phones and mobile phone accessories,
into speech marks. This treatment is brilliantly relevant to
Talkmore's business name and industry. Notice how most of
the design is created in black and white, with just enough color
added to call attention to the clever transformation of letters
into speech marks. This is a classic example of how text does
not have to be lifeless.

talkmore

By nido

2001

talkmore™

**New Bedford
Whaling Museum**

By Malcolm Grear
Designers

2005

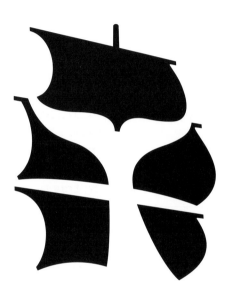

NEW BEDFORD
WHALING
MUSEUM

Commit to memory

A solid iconic design is one that onlookers will remember after just one quick glance. Think, for instance, of passengers traveling on a bus, looking out the window and noticing a billboard as the bus whizzes past. Or what about pedestrians, looking up just as a branded truck drives by. Quite often, one quick glance is all the time you get to make an impression.

But how do you focus on this one element of iconic design? It sometimes helps to think about the logos that you remember most when you sit down at the drawing table. What is it about them that keeps them ingrained in your memory? It also helps to limit how much time you spend on each sketch idea—try 30 seconds. Otherwise, how can you expect an onlooker to remember it with a quick glance? You want viewers' experience with your client's brand identity to be such that the logo is remembered the instant they see it the next time.

Malcolm Grear Designers worked with the New Bedford Whaling Museum to craft its brand identity. The museum is the largest in America devoted to the history of the American whaling industry at a time when sailing ships dominated merchant trade and whaling. By combining boat sails with the tail fin of a whale, and employing a unique use of negative space, the resulting design reflects the idea of "whaling in the age of sail."

Think small

As much as you might want to see your work plastered across billboards, don't forget your design may also need to accommodate smaller, yet necessary, applications, such as zipper pulls and clothing labels. Clients are usually enthusiastic about, and demanding of, an adaptable logo, since it can save them a substantial amount of money on printing costs, brand implementation meetings, potential redesigns, and more.

In creating a versatile design, simplicity is key. Your design should ideally work at a minimum size of around one inch, without loss of detail. The only way to accomplish this is to keep it simple, which will also increase your chances of hitting on a design that is likely to last.

Sugoi

By Rethink
Communications

Creative director:
Ian Grais /
Chris Staples

Designer:
Nancy Wu

2007

Nancy Wu, a designer in Vancouver, British Columbia, came up with this brand identity for Sugoi, a 20-year-old technical cycling apparel company founded in Vancouver. Over the years, the brand had evolved to embrace runners and triathletes, so the company wanted a renewed icon, one with an extra nod toward active lifestyle brands.

Sugoi context

2007

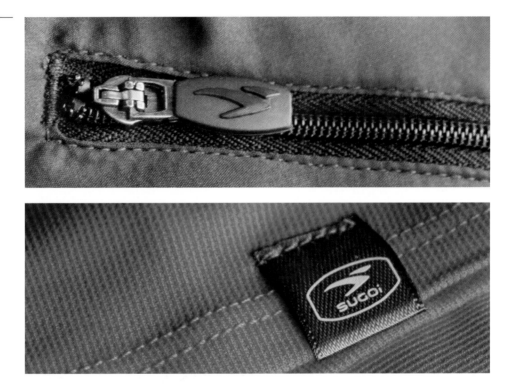

The logo symbolizes a stylized *s*-shaped figure, striving ahead, communicating the brand's forward momentum and representing core strength emanating from within. Supported by custom typography, this modern icon embodies energy, boldness, technical innovation, and quality.

Focus on one thing

Iconic designs that stand apart from the crowd have just one feature to help them stand out. That's it. Just one. Not two, three, or four. You want to leave your client with just one thing to remember about your design. As I've touched on already, your client's customers won't spend a lot of time studying the logo. Usually, one quick glance, and they're gone.

In 2008, the brand identity for the French Property Exhibition was in need of a makeover. The exhibition is the largest property event in the United Kingdom for people who are interested in buying homes in France. Executives at *French Property News*, the U.K.-based French-property publication that organizes the event, felt that the original logo was no longer appropriate. It was more reminiscent of a French bistro than a major exhibition event. The angle of the brushstrokes was a distortion of the French tricolor. And the type felt somewhat frivolous.

English-based designer Roy Smith was given the task of redesigning the logo.

"I explored various directions in the form of thumbnail sketches—a vital part of the conceptualization process. The French flag, rooftops, and louvred shutters—very much a French icon," said Smith.

His final concept makes use of the French flag, but focuses on one relevant attribute of property—the open door, welcoming everyone in.

French Property Exhibition

By Roy Smith Design

2008

The old logo (left) and Smith's new design (right)

It's French. It's property.

Brilliant.

Roy could have added another mark to the design, perhaps something reminiscent of the Eiffel Tower. After all, everyone would immediately equate a symbol like the Eiffel Tower with France. But then the viewer would have been forced to consider an unnecessary element, which would make the design less memorable.

"The new design is an evolution of the French tricolor. It can be interpreted as open shutters or an open door, subtly welcoming visitors. It also resembles the exhibition panels themselves," said Smith. "With three lines of type, I decided to use the evenly weighted Avenir regular in caps, to keep it flush with the clean lines of the mark."

The seven ingredients in your signature dish

We've talked about the elements that should be part of your iconic designs, and we've looked at a few worthy examples to back them up. How memorable are these elements for you now? Since they're not as easy to remember as a brilliant minimal black-and-white design, it might help to do a quick review:

- **Keep it simple.** The simplest solution is often the most effective. Why? Because a simple logo helps meet most of the other requirements of iconic design.
- **Make it relevant.** Any logo you design must be appropriate for the business it identifies. For example, as much as you might want to use a fun design that makes everyone smile, this approach is not ideal for businesses like the local crematorium.
- **Incorporate tradition.** Trends come and go like the wind. With brand identity, the last thing you want is to invest a significant amount of your time and your client's money in a design direction that looks dated almost overnight.
- **Aim for distinction.** Begin by focusing on a design that is recognizable. So recognizable, in fact, that just its shape or outline gives it away.

- **Commit to memory.** Quite often, one quick glance is all the time you get to make an impression. You want your viewers' experience to be such that your logo is remembered the instant they see it the next time.
- **Think small.** Your design should ideally work at a minimum of around one inch in size without loss of detail so that it can be put to use for many different applications.
- **Focus on one thing.** Incorporate just one feature to help your designs stand out. That's it. Just one. Not two, three, or four.

Remember that rules are made to be broken

By sticking to the rules for creating iconic designs, you stand a greater chance of delivering timeless and enduring logos that leave your clients buzzing. But can you do more? And do you always need to play by the book? Keep in mind that rules are made to be broken. It's up to you to tread new paths and break through the boundaries in your attempts to create designs that are a cut above the rest. Whether your results are successful will obviously be open to question, but you'll learn so much more and so much faster when any potential mistakes are your own, rather than someone else's.

Part II

The process of design

Chapter four

Laying the groundwork

At some point down the road, you may find yourself educating your client about design, but first you must educate yourself about your client. Without knowing the nitty-gritty details of your client's business, his reasons for seeking a brand identity, and expectations of the process and the final design, you cannot possibly be successful.

Gathering these details takes a significant investment of time, and more than a little patience, especially when you're itching to get started on the fun part—the act of designing. But if you scrimp on the time and attention required at this early stage and dive right into the design work, you risk completely missing your client's mark.

Shaking out the jitters

At the onset of just about any design project, you or your client, or sometimes both of you, will likely be feeling some anxiety. That's because, as any designer with a bit of experience can attest, the client-designer relationship doesn't always run smoothly.

For your part, you need to be careful choosing clients, in the same way that clients often choose from a number of designers. Always remember that you're being hired because you're the expert. The client should not assume the role of telling you what to do. He should be comfortable simply letting you do what you do best—create iconic brand identities.

If you feel uneasy in any way about the relationship, you should definitely find a way to discuss it with the client. There's nothing like healthy dialogue to get a clear sense of what is expected, both on your part and on the part of your client.

Most clients will be anxious about the process of having a brand identity created for their business. They see ideas as a risk, and not as a way to secure their mortgage. So the more indepth your initial discussions, the more at ease you will make your clients. It may be that it's their first time working on an identity project, and it's up to you to show them how smoothly the process can flow.

It's all in the design brief

Understanding your client's motivations involves a lot more than simply setting minds at ease, however. You're not a mind reader, so a series of very specific questions and answers about your client's needs and desires is the first order of business. You then turn this information into a design brief that reflects the expectations of both you and your client for the project.

The design brief plays a pivotal role in guiding both you and the client to an effective outcome. There may be stumbling blocks that crop up along the way—your client may disagree with a decision you've made, for instance. It's at points like this when you can return to the details of the brief to back up your stance.

That's not to say you won't make design changes as a result of a disagreement—you want to please your client, after all. But the design brief exists to provide both of you with concrete reasons for making decisions throughout the design process.

There are several ways you might obtain the information you need from your client: by telephone, video chat, in person, or by email. I find that with many of my clients, it's useful to pose questions in the form of an online questionnaire or email. With others, I might feel that more face-to-face time is necessary. What matters most is that you're able to extract as much relevant information as possible, and at the beginning of the process.

Gathering preliminary information

You'll want to note the following basic information before posing your more indepth questions:

- The organization's name
- Its location
- Number of years in business
- Number of employees
- The product or service sold
- The challenges faced
- Who the competitors are

In addition, you need to determine who the decision-maker is and whether you will be dealing directly with that person throughout the project. Dealing with the decision-maker—in other words, the person or committee who has the final say over the company's brand identity—isn't as critical during the information-gathering stage as it is when you present your ideas. We'll talk more about this in Chapter 8.

When working with larger organizations, it will be likely that your point of contact is an employee, rather than the CEO or marketing director. This person will help you to gather all the necessary information to be included in the design brief. Later in the process, he most likely will introduce you to the decision-maker or a committee. But for now, the focus is on information gathering.

Asking the tougher questions

The crux of a healthy design brief lies in the questions you pose. Obtaining this information isn't difficult. You just need to ask.

What follows are some suggested questions to use as a starting point. Keep in mind, however, as you form your own list, that the needs of each industry and every company vary.

What does your audience care about?

Asking this question not only helps focus and orient your creative efforts around what appeals to your client's customers, but it also shows that you have an interest in your client's customers, and not a simple wish to please personal tastes.

How do people learn about your product, organization, or service?

Knowing how your client reaches out to its customer base will help you picture how and where the new logo will be used. This knowledge will affect the type of design you suggest and ultimately create. If the company promotes itself via leaflets at trade events, you might remind the decision-maker that his multicolor rainbow effect will cost more to produce than, say, a cool gray monotone design. Having an understanding of the client's promotional strategies not only allows you to play a role in helping the company stay on track, but also enables you to deliver a cost-effective design that works on many levels.

Why does your audience need a new brand identity?

In answering this question, your client is forced to articulate why a new identity design is necessary. Sometimes companies are reacting to their competitors—a rival may have launched a new visual system, for instance—and the company wants to respond by doing the same. In this case, encourage your client to proceed slowly and cautiously, and refrain from responding to a gut reaction. The company may have built enormous equity around a strong and longstanding brand identity, so it's vital not to disregard it entirely and all at once.

A better idea might be to refine or refresh the current system, rather than opt for a complete overhaul. We'll talk more about this in the next chapter.

What words do you want people to associate with your company?

You may want to suggest a few adjectives, such as "creative," "professional," "traditional," or "playful," to help get your client started. The replies can direct you towards specific styles of design.

Generally, what logos do you think will appeal to your customers, and why?

By switching the focus away from your client's individual design tastes and onto those of the customer, you keep the process aimed at the good of the company as a whole, and not just the personal preference of one person.

How many people are responsible for use of the brand identity?

It's important for your client to keep a tight reign over the use of the work you create. As an extreme example, you don't want a low resolution "saved for web" logo file to be enlarged and used on the cover of a printed sales manual. It defeats the purpose of hiring a specialist. By asking this question, you invite a followup conversation about the importance of brand guidelines. You might even, at some point, offer to create a logo style guide that illustrates for the company how to use, and *not* use, the design.

Give your client time and space

These questions will be enough to get you started. You likely will have more to add, given that every industry has its own specific requirements, quirks, and expectations.

As you pose your set of questions, make sure that you don't rush the client to answer them. We all appreciate some space to consider answers in our own time, and you'll end up gaining more insight, too. Welcome the opportunity to answer seemingly off-topic questions, because at this stage every detail helps.

But maintain the focus

In addition, don't allow your client to confuse this as a chance to dictate terms; instead it's an opportunity to really focus on the project, and on the benefits the outcome will achieve. It's precisely this level of focus that will provide you with all of the information you need to do your job.

The answers you're provided should spur some ongoing discussion about design ideas.

Homework time

Once you've gathered all of the preliminary information you've sought, spend some time very carefully reviewing it. What are your client's concerns?

What does the company want to play up? What is it truly selling? And how does the company want to present itself in the market? Logos that are pretty may win awards, but they don't always win marketshare.

The next step of the information-gathering stage involves conducting your own field research. Learn as much as you can about the company, its history, its current brand identity and the effect it has had on market perception. And don't forget to review any brand identities it has used in the past. These additional insights are critical. You also need to focus on how your client's competitors have branded themselves, picking up on any weaknesses you perceive and using them to your advantage in your design. After all, if your client is to win, there needs to be a loser.

Assembling the design brief

Documenting the information can be a matter of taking notes during a meeting (having a minute taker present can be a big help), recording telephone conversations, editing an email back-and-forth, and stripping the chat down to just the meaty parts. Did I mention that designers need to be editors, too?

It's wise to create a succinct, easily accessed, and easily shared document that you or your client can refer to at any time. You'll want to send a copy to those involved in the project. And keep a copy in hand to use in followup meetings.

For your part, you want to use the brief to help you keep your designs focused. I'm sure that I'm not the only designer to have ever entertained some pretty far-fetched ideas every now and then. Relevancy—one of the elements we've already discussed—is key, and your brief can help you stay on track.

Let's look at a few instances in which designers extracted critical information from their clients and then used it to create very effective results.

A mission and some objectives hold the key

Clive's is a specialist organic bakery set in the heart of Devon, England. Since 1986, the company has been making pies stuffed to the bursting point with unique fillings inspired by culinary traditions from around the world.

In 2005, Clive's asked English studio biz-R to rebrand Clive's (at the time the company was named Buckfast Organic Bakery) because its existing identity had become dated, inconsistent, and uninspiring. The brand was also failing to communicate the vibrancy behind the company and its unique range of vegetarian and gluten-free pies, cakes, and pastries.

biz-R got the creative process rolling by creating a design brief that included a description of Clive's mission, as well as the project's objectives.

The mission was to contemporize the bakery's image and emphasize the uniqueness of the product. The new brand objectives aimed to communicate the dynamic personality of the company, highlight the organic nature of the products and their homemade quality, convey the healthy, yet fun and tasty recipes, and introduce Clive's to a new generation of health-conscious, brand-aware consumers.

Clive's

By biz-R

2005

biz-R's solution was to create a logo that combined a handrawn typeface with clean modern type, communicating the forward-thinking values of the company, together with the homemade qualities of the products.

The strapline "made with love" emphasizes the handmade, healthy, natural, and organic quality of Clive's products.

The company wanted Clive's new identity applied to its packaging, marketing materials, website, and company vehicles. Biz-R created a new design for the packaging that combined the logo with "Pot of" typography and colorful graphics.

Clive's

Clive's implemented its new identity across the entire business.

Large, distinctive typography, bright colors, and bold photography focusing on fresh organic ingredients make the brand easily identifiable, giving it a contemporary, confident appearance and appealing to a much wider audience than before.

Field research to the rescue

When Federal Express Corporation invented the overnight shipping business in 1973, the market was one-dimensional: one country (USA), one package type (letter), and one delivery time (10:30 a.m.). By 1992, the company had added new services (end of next business day, and two-day economy) and was shipping packages and freight to 186 countries. But by then, a host of competitors had emerged and created the perception of a commodity industry driven by price. As the most expensive service, Federal Express was losing market share.

Federal Express Corporation

An earlier brand identity

The company clearly needed to better communicate its broad service offering and reaffirm its position as the industry leader. It hired global design firm Landor in 1994 to create a new brand identity that would help reposition the delivery corporation.

For Landor, market research was key in producing an enduring and effective design. Landor and Federal Express assigned both their internal research groups to collaborate for a nine-month global research study. The study revealed that businesses and consumers were unaware of the global scope and full-service capabilities offered by FedEx, believing that the company shipped only overnight and only within the United States.

Landor conducted additional research about the Federal Express name itself. It found that many people negatively associated the word "federal" with government and bureaucracy, and the word "express" was overused. In the United States alone, over 900 company names were employing this word.

On a more upbeat note for Federal Express, the research also revealed that businesses and consumers had been shortening the company's name and turning it into a generic verb—as in "I need to FedEx a package," regardless which shipper was being used. In addition, research questions posed to the company's target audience confirmed that the shortened form of the name, "FedEx," conveyed a greater sense of speed, technology, and innovation than the formal name.

Landor advised Federal Express senior management to adopt "FedEx" as its communicative name—to better communicate the breadth of its services—while retaining "Federal Express Corporation" as the full legal name of the organization.

Over 300 designs were created in the exploratory phase, ranging from evolutionary (developed from the original) to revolutionary (altogether different concepts).

FedEx logo options

Preliminary design 1

Preliminary design 2

Preliminary design 3

The new visual identity and abbreviated company name that Landor designed allows for greater consistency and impact in different applications, ranging from packages and drop boxes to vehicles, aircraft, customer service centers, and uniforms.

Federal Express Corporation

By Lindon Leader (while at Landor)

1994

Landor and FedEx spent a great deal of time and energy researching the marketplace, discovering how the Federal Express brand was perceived, where they needed to improve, and how to do it. This is a fine example in which indepth preparation led to an iconic solution.

Bringing the details of client discussions to life

Designer Maggie Macnab was asked to create a new logo for the Heart Hospital of New Mexico. As a teacher who has taught brand identity at the University of New Mexico for more than 10 years and is a past president of the Communication Artists of New Mexico, Maggie felt it was vital to clarify her client's expectations from the very outset.

During the information gathering stage, Maggie had meetings with the hospital design committee (comprising doctors from merging small practices and the funding insurance company). She asked what was required from the brand project, and was given these criteria:

- The identity must have a New Mexico "look and feel."
- It must (obviously) be directly related to cardiology.
- The patients need to know that they're in very good hands.

Broader research on New Mexico told Maggie that the Zia symbol was being used as the state logo, and had been for more than 100 years. The Zia are an indigenous tribe centered at Zia Pueblo, an Indian reservation in New Mexico. They are known for their pottery and the use of the Zia emblem. Zia Pueblo claims this design; it's a prevalent indigenous pictograph found in the New Mexico area.

The Zia sun symbol

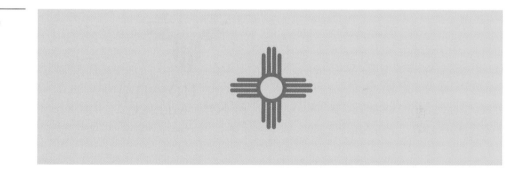

"I knew there was something about all three project criteria in the Zia symbol, so I encouraged the doctors to ask for an audience with the elders at Zia Pueblo to request the use of their identifying mark," said Maggie. "The Zia is an ancient and sacred design, and I was well aware of Zia Pueblo's issue with people randomly slapping it on the side of any old work truck as an identity, which happens often in New Mexico."

After dozens of experimental iterations and sketches, Maggie integrated the palm of a hand with a heart shape, and the Zia became the mark symbolizing both New Mexico and the ministering of hands-on care.

Heart Hospital of New Mexico

By
Maggie Macnab

1998

HEART HOSPITAL
of NEW MEXICO

Maggie's thoroughness during the initial project stages not only convinced Zia Pueblo to grant the use of the Zia symbol, but they also blessed the hospital grounds and danced at the groundbreaking ceremony. Excellent PR for the fledgling heart hospital.

"It's always a good idea to be sensitive to things like this," added Maggie. "Not only are you doing the right thing by showing common courtesy, but respecting traditions and differences can bring great and unexpected things together— very important for collective acceptance."

Culling the adjectives supplied by the client

Earlier in the chapter, I mentioned the importance of asking clients which words they want people to associate with their brand identity. This can be very fruitful information for a designer.

Executives at Harned, Bachert & Denton (HBD), a law firm in Bowling Green, Kentucky, felt that HBD's brand identity didn't effectively portray the experience, history, and integrity that the firm had built over nearly 20 years. They wanted a logo that distinguished them as a professional and unified group of ethical attorneys.

Harned, Bachert & Denton, LLP

Old logo design

The old HBD monogram lacked any sense of design style and was very easy to forget, so designer Stephen Lee Ogden was given the task of creating an effective redesign. Meetings, chats, and email between client and design team helped Stephen learn what was needed for the new identity.

The following words were specified as the ideal fit: professional, ethical, strong, competent, unified, relevant, experienced, detail-oriented, and approachable. Ogden relied heavily on these adjectives to help him shape the new icon.

Harned Bachert & Denton, LLP

By Stephen Lee Ogden, during employment at Earnhart+Friends of Bowling Green, Kentucky

2007

HARNED BACHERT
& DENTON LLP

The rational behind the icon was that the simple, bold shape would come to symbolize a unified firm. All of the firm's partners bought into the idea.

When you take the time up front to really get to know your client and the related industry, you not only stand a much greater chance of delivering a design you respect and they love, but you also place yourself in an optimal position for educating them about designs at some point down the road. Once they see what you're made of, they may start to really listen to your feedback and even follow your lead.

HBD business card design

Contemporary and professional, the mark works equally well without the accompanying business name.

Chapter five

Skirting the hazards of a redesign

When clients approach designers for brand identity projects, the projects generally fall into one of two categories. They either represent a newly established company in need of a new identity, or an already established company that desires a redesigned or refined brand identity.

If your project falls into the first category—designing from scratch—the process is much simpler, since there's no brand equity for the designer and client to consider. But if you've been asked to do a redesign, the stakes are much higher, for both you and your client. Think about it. Which scenario is potentially more damaging: Nike ditching its internationally recognized "swoosh" logo in favor of, say, the outline of a shoe, or a new business named "Pete's" comissioning a visual identity to help sell its custom t-shirts? Because of Nike's stature, stock, and visibility in the marketplace, the potential for damage to the company's identity is much greater.

That said, a redesign project tends to be much more lucrative for the designer than creating a design from scratch. Because established companies need to be protective of the equity they have already built around their identity, a lengthier, more stringent design process is required. Every decision requires more thought, and more discussion.

What are the reasons for rebranding?

While the lure of a high-paying redesign might initially seem like a win-win, it's critical that you understand from the outset why your client is looking to rebrand. It's not unusual to find that a company hopes the buzz associated with the new identity will increase its sales in the short term. But rebranding simply for the sake of it or to follow the latest trends can result in disaster. It's up to you to talk with your clients about the specific reasons for their projects, and advise them about which course of action makes the most sense. Without this type of guidance, market leaders can end up throwing millions away, and your reputation with it.

Let's take a look at an instance in which designing a new brand identity to replace a well-established one had unintended and punishing consequences.

Don't squeeze too hard

In 2009, PepsiCo attempted to stimulate sales of its premium fruit juice brand Tropicana by hiring the Arnell Group to redesign its packaging. PepsiCo and the Arnell Group thought it would be a good idea to give Tropicana's brand identity some new energy, and make it more relevant to the times, said Peter Arnell, founder and CEO of the Arnell Group.

"We had always depicted the outside of an orange. What was fascinating was that we had never actually shown the product—the juice itself," said Arnell.

Tropicana's former and current identity (left) and unsuccessful rebranded identity (right)

Photo by Brian Alexander Gray

2008

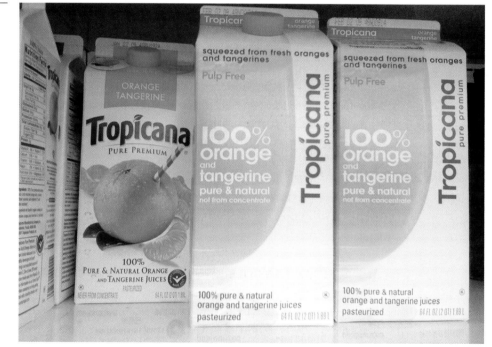

Those who are familiar with the Tropicana brand know that PepsiCo for years had used the "straw stuck in an orange" symbol to promote the premium juice product. Consumers were used to it—those who were loyal customers of the brand could easily spot the packaging when they went grocery shopping.

It goes without saying that hindsight is a wonderful thing, but was it really necessary to visually remind Tropicana's customers what this product called juice looked like?

In comparing the two identities, it's obvious that the redesign is definitely a more diluted identity—it has an almost generic look to it. The full brand name is Tropicana Pure Premium, so perhaps this dilution of the brand equity was a conscious decision on the part of the company and designer. According to the Private Label Manufacturers Association, one of every five items sold today in the United States is what's considered a "generic" store brand.[1]

Despite the fact that Tropicana is considered a premium juice, maybe the company wanted to align its product with the more generic juice packaging of store labels?

Whatever the case, the rebranding didn't work. After the new packaging was put on supermarket shelves, sales of the Tropicana Pure Premium line plummeted 20 percent in less than two months,[2] costing PepsiCo $33 million in lost sales.[3] Within two months of unveiling the new identity in early 2009, the company bowed to consumer demand by reverting to the old packaging.

[1] Private Label Manufacturers' Association. "Store Brands Achieving New Heights of Consumer Popularity and Growth," http://plma.com/storeBrands/sbt09.html
[2] AdAge.com. "Tropicana Line's Sales Plunge 20% Post-Rebranding," April 2, 2009.
[3] BrandingStrategyInsider.com. "Tropicana's Costly Listening Lesson," April 15, 2009, www.brandingstrategyinsider.com/2009/04/tropicanas-costly-lesson-in-listening-.html

"New Coke" packaging in 1985 rebranding effort

When emotions run high

The Tropicana rebranding is a great testimony to the emotional attachment that customers can have to a brand. Another apt example is the "new Coke" rebranding way back in 1985.

Do you remember it? Coca-Cola changed both the design on the can and the taste of the soft drink in the hopes that a revitalized product would boost sales and attract new customers. The result? Less than three months after the introduction of "new Coke," more than 400,000[4] consumers called or wrote letters to complain.

Despite the fact that sales of Coke had increased 8 percent over the same month a year earlier,[5] pressure from a minority of disgruntled customers—albeit a huge minority, if there is such a thing—forced Coca-Cola executives to announce a return to the original drink formula.

The upside of the debacle? Even though the change provoked nearly half a million complaints, the uproar generated huge interest in the brand.

[4] Constance L. Hayes, *The Real Thing: Truth and Power at the Coca-Cola Company*, (New York: Random House, 2004), p. 119.
[5] John S. Demott, Joseph J. Kane, and Charles Pelton, "All Afizz Over the New Coke," *Time* 125 no. 25 (June 24, 1985), www.time.com/time/magazine/article/0,9171,959449,00.html.

Was this a purposeful ploy on the part of the company to gain media attention, or a genuine mistake that could easily have generated a huge loss? I don't know. But what I do know is that for us creatures of habit, change does not come easily. So if you are working on a rebranding project for a client, be sure that the reasons for the redesign are sound.

Answers often lie in focus groups

Both the Tropicana and "new Coke" rebranding projects are likely cases in which conducting some focus groups would have provided valuable clues about the risks of changing the packaging.

When you are working on a project in which a client with a well-established brand identity is seeking a redesign, you should ask very early in the process whether any focus groups have been studied to establish the need. If they have not, you might suggest that quizzing existing and potential customers about their perceptions of the brand should be the first order of business.

Some designers and agencies offer to set up focus groups as part of their services. If you feel that your schedule can't accommodate such an endeavor, or focus group research just isn't your thing, you might consider bringing a specialist onboard to get the job done.

Of course, most brand designs do not turn out as poorly as these examples, and both PepsiCo and Coca-Cola have likely experienced other successful redesigns of their products.

Let's now examine a very justified and well-planned redesign project.

From "unresponsive" to "caring"

Design firm Leader Creative was given the task of rebranding CIGNA Corporation. The CIGNA brand encompasses an array of services, ranging from reinsurance, property, and casualty insurance to health care delivery and investment services. CIGNA executives approached Leader Creative because the company was not convinced its existing brand identity conveyed just how wide-ranging its services actually are.

CIGNA and Leader Creative first conducted focus groups in the United States and seven other countries. They discovered that CIGNA customers were generally unaware of the broad range of products and services in CIGNA's portfolio, and that little cross-selling existed among the 10 highly diversified and independent business units.

Respondents in the research study didn't see the existing "blue box" wordmark or the clinical, business-to-business tagline, "We get paid for results," as displaying any of the desired attributes the company hoped they would see. Instead, many of them said they thought the brand identity pictured the company as "bureaucratic" and "unresponsive." Ouch.

CIGNA's former "blue box" logo

CIGNA determined its businesses would derive more benefit from a single umbrella brand, as long as the brand conveyed the desired attributes: caring, strength, and stability.

Wary of abandoning the brand equity that CIGNA had built around its old identity, Leader Creative first experimented with design options that kept the "blue box" on board, but attempted to add a sense of energy to help overcome the unresponsive tag.

What happened, however, was that these designs scored poorly in qualitative research for two reasons: The acronym had no apparent meaning, and constituents, particularly in the health care division, were looking for an emotional connection and a sense of security.

CIGNA logo explorations

Options 1 and 2

By
Leader Creative

So Leader Creative went back to the drawing board to work on other ideas. One of them involved the use of a tree, which came about by further developing thoughts of growth, strength, and stability. Two of those words are ones that the company expressed as desirable attributes; and all three relate to the use of a tree as a symbol.

CIGNA's new brand identity

By
Leader Creative

1993

"The new 'Tree of Life' identity and the slogan 'A Business of Caring' provided CIGNA with an image that portrays the company as thoughtful, caring, and responsive, while still maintaining the attributes of professionalism, stability, and strength," said Lindon Leader, founder of Leader Creative.

The incorporation of one main umbrella brand helped CIGNA simplify thousands of company forms, and broadened audience appreciation of the diverse, full-service organization.

Maybe just some tweaking?

Sometimes, however, a full redesign might mean going a step too far when all that's needed is a refinement of the design—some tweaks here and there that still retain the equity behind the visual. Refinement is a good option when your client's identity has become a little dated over the years, but consumers' familiarity with the identity is high.

JCJ Architecture, a U.S.-based design firm that provides architectural and interior services for public and private clients in the education, hospitality, and corporate realms, commissioned designer Armin Vit of UnderConsideration to refresh its brand identity. The company needed not only an updated identity, but one that could also easily conform to any number of marketing applications.

The firm's old logotype made use of the venerable Helvetica Neue, and was used in all of JCJ's identity materials.

JCJ Architecture former brand identity

JCJARCHITECTURE

Helvetica Neue is a type family that was digitized in 1983 and is based on the design of the original and popular Helvetica, created in 1957. Except for some overly tight kerning, there's nothing dramatically wrong with JCJ Architecture's old logotype—Helvetica Neue is a well-crafted typeface. But there was a period in the early nineties when it seemed like every new design used it. Armin Vit agreed with his client that a typeface rooted in the 21st century was in order.

JCJ Architecture new brand identity

By Armin Vit for Under Consideration

2008

JCJARCHITECTURE

**JCJ Architecture
stationery design**

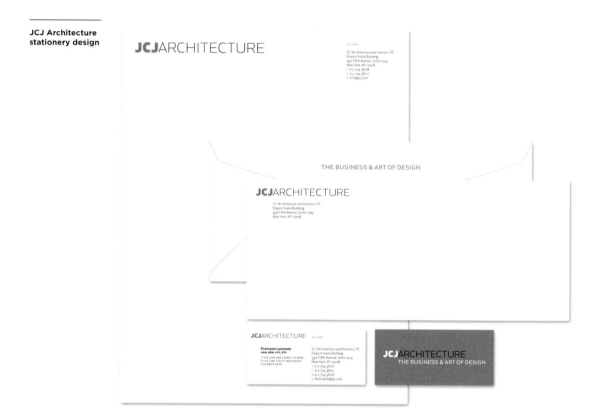

The design works because it helps JCJ stand out from all those other Helvetica Neue logos and modernizes the client's visual identity. It establishes consistency and allows for flexibility in printing methods, whether they are full-bleed brochures printed offset or bordered printouts from the office laser printer. The distinctive red color of the lettering was retained, so the brand equity built around the old design remains intact.

Remember your manners

In questioning your client about the reasons for a redesign, don't forget your manners when sharing your impressions of the current brand—it might just be that the business owner designed it herself. Ask instead whether the company believes the current image is doing the successful company justice, and then focus on the positives of what you can bring to the table. Good designers are good salespeople, too.

Chapter six

Pricing design

The age-old question of, "How much should I charge my clients for identity design?" is one that every designer struggles with at some point. So if you don't know what your skills are worth, rest assured you're not alone. I still wonder whether I'm doing myself justice with the rates I've set, and I've been in charge of my business for what seems like a very long time.

You cannot accurately price a design project without first understanding the needs of your client. Designers who advertise a list of predetermined prices for *x* amount of concepts with *x* rounds of revisions are attempting to commoditize a profession that by definition cannot be commoditized.

Every client is different, so every design project will be, too. It makes no sense to pigeonhole your clients into a specific price bracket. What works for one will not work for another, and your time—and profits—take a big hit when you limit yourself to a set range and attract clients on the basis of price alone.

The design pricing formula

Pricing design is far from an exact science, and even when you think you've covered every possible factor for determining your costs, another one will crop up and force you to recalculate. But it's still important to consider what affects the amount you quote, and how you can ensure you actually make a profit.

Pricing generally varies depending on a number of factors:

- Your level of expertise
- Project specification
- Expected turnaround time
- Additional service and support
- Level of demand
- Current economy

Let's take a closer look.

Your level of expertise

Only you can determine how much your skills are worth, and this value is the result of your experience in dealing with clients. I frequently ask myself if I'm charging too much or charging too little, and I reckon every other designer does too. But the main goal is to make sure you're adequately compensated for your level of experience and education; your reputation; the overhead you incur for office space, equipment, electricity and heating, health care, and living costs; and the expenses you will incur as a result of working through the design project with your client (travel costs, your time, and so on). Clearly these elements will differ from person to person.

Project specification

Let's say you're working with two clients at the same time. One is a local shoe store owner who is just launching his first business, and the other is a 500-person-strong multinational company that has been in business for 50 years and needs a rebrand. You won't need to research the shoe store's company history. Nor will you need to draft an identity style guide, since most likely just the owner will be dealing with the application of your design. And you won't be booking international flights for brand meetings. So the shoe store project will obviously cost you and your client less than the multinational company project. As much as I'd love to give you specific figures, only you can determine how much less.

Expected turnaround time

If a client is under pressure to have a job completed within a tight time frame, you should consider applying a "rush job" markup to the project. Accepting the request means that you, too, will be under increased pressure to get the job done, and might result in a rescheduling of your existing projects. I recommend a markup of 20 percent to 50 percent, depending on the urgency of the deadline.

Additional service and support

When a client needs a new website to go along with her new logo, consider it an opportunity, even if such a service falls outside your skill set. It's situations like these that allow you to provide that extra level of service and support that is most useful to your client.

You can approach other designers—those who specialize in web design and development—to see if they might be able to provide the needed service. Then negotiate a finder's fee with the designer, whereby each project you send his way equates to a percentage of the total bill. My subcontractors and I find that 10 or 15 percent is a fair cut.

You might even want to start a partnership with these designers, creating a new business identity that shares project responsibility and potentially attracts larger, more lucrative clients.

Something to think about.

Level of demand

Let's say you're snowed under with work. Your project calendar is filled for the next six months with a steady stream of clients, yet you still receive new inquiries and are reluctant to turn them away. This is your opportunity to significantly raise your rates. If the client says no, it's not hurting your bottom line, but if the client says yes, you're happy to put in some overtime because you're being adequately compensated and can look forward to rewarding yourself when the project is complete.

Put simply, if lots of clients are demanding your design services, it's time to charge more, because this is a sign that you're worth it.

Current economy

You will find that many company owners and CEOs are reluctant to spend large amounts on design during an economic downturn, so you might discover there are less inquiries about hiring you. Some designers will lower their rates as a result, but my advice is to charge what you normally do, because there will be smart clients out there who wisely see the downturn as an ideal time to spend on branding. When competitors are cutting back, there's a great opportunity to increase market share by attracting new customers.

If you find business hard to come by in tougher economic times, don't take it as a prompt to lower your rates. Instead, use it as an opportunity to improve your own marketing methods. Why not give your portfolio a more professional edge? Or draft a list of potential companies you can target with a sales drive? That way, when the market swings, you'll be in a much stronger position to take advantage of it.

Comparing the design profession to any other is by no means exact, but the, "How much for a logo?" question is a little like asking a real estate agent, "How much for a house?"

Hourly rates or a set fee?

When supplying potential clients with quotes for brand identity design, you can provide either a set fee for the entire project, or an hourly rate multiplied by the number of hours you anticipate the project will take.

It may seem like a difficult choice, but it's not if you really think about it. First, put yourself in the client's shoes. Would you prefer to know beforehand exactly what a project will cost, or would you opt for an hourly rate whereby the project could take longer than anticipated and risk running up a huge bill? Nearly all clients would prefer a set fee.

Now look at how the choice can affect your profits. You've spent $100,000 on a design education, spanning five years of your life, so that you're able to accomplish in just a matter of minutes or hours what once took weeks or months. In the words of brand identity designer Paula Scher, "It took me a few seconds to draw it, but it took me 34 years to learn how to draw it in a few seconds."

If you attempt to quantify what you're worth into an hourly figure, you will either send your potential client to another designer because he doesn't believe you're worth it, or you will unwittingly undervalue your talent in order to clinch a deal.

The choice is easy. You offer a set fee.

Tell your client that you would charge *x* amount for the project. If you start mentioning hours, you may find the client deeming particular tasks unnecessary, wondering if eliminating certain tasks will both speed the process and save money.

The reality is that you can only determine an exact time frame after the project has started and when the true scope of what's involved becomes apparent, so an hourly time allocation will always be destined to change. Again, your clients will be happier if they don't have unexpected costs, so a set fee wins every time.

When discussing time frames, always aim to under-promise and over-deliver. If you think a particular task will take two weeks, say it's three. This way you're compensating for any unforeseen mishaps, and, if all goes according to plan, you will delight your client by delivering ahead of schedule.

Handling print costs

A brand identity design project is likely to contain a range of print design, such as business cards, letterhead paper, or a promotional brochure, but it can be difficult to determine how and what to charge your client for providing this service.

Designers and design studios normally charge a markup on the total print costs when they handle this service for the client. This is their way of recouping the time and effort spent liaising with the print company. There's no industry standard percentage, but somewhere between a 15 and 25 percent markup is a good starting point.

To put it simply, if a project requires you to supply your client with a small promotional brochure, and your commercial printer says it will cost you $10,000 for the print run, then you should consider charging your client between $11,500 and $12,500 (not including design costs—where you will be making the majority of your profits). And keep in mind that unless you have a long-established relationship with the printer, you will probably need to pay for printing in advance.

My preference is to advise clients to deal directly with a local printer. This helps clients in two ways: They save money that is otherwise spent on my markup, and they build a business relationship with someone local, which can save a significant amount of money on future print runs. And if your clients take the time to ask a printer how to make the most of the money they plan to spend on their printing project, they likely will be surprised at the advice and help the printer delivers. Printers love it when they're involved in the process, because it saves them and their customers a lot of headaches.

However, your clients won't always want to deal directly with a printer, which raises the question, "How can you pay the printer in advance when you haven't received any money from your client?" This leads us nicely to the next piece of advice.

Receipt of a down payment

It is essential that you receive a down payment prior to commencing work—especially when dealing with a client with whom you have no prior relationship. If you don't get one, it's easy to be taken for a ride.

I made a mistake of falling into this trap in my early days of self-employment. I once worked with a client with whom I had an understanding that full payment would be made after I sent my initial design ideas. I dutifully supplied my client with the designs, but almost immediately after, my client contact evaporated, and I was left with nothing.

I asked Jonathan Selikoff of New Jersey-based design studio Selikoff+Company how he normally charges his clients.

"It depends on the client and the relationship, but initially, all my projects are based on a flat fee, per project basis, with a defined scope," said Selikoff.

"I usually ask for a third or 50 percent of the fee up front, depending on the size of the fee. Hourly rates never benefit anyone. The client doesn't get a true idea of the value of the work and risks getting overcharged. I prefer to deliver a desired outcome, not work for *x* amount of hours and hope for the best. If it takes too long to achieve the goal, then I either underpriced the service, or I didn't work efficiently enough, neither of which is something the client should suffer from."

I, too, normally ask for a 50 percent deposit of the total fee prior to starting the project. Getting this payment up front helps in two ways: First, I'm ensured that my time is compensated for, and second, the client has that additional source of motivation to see the project through to completion.

The money exchange

After having worked with overseas clients for some time, I began to wonder about fluctuations in exchange rates, and whether I should factor these into my initial quotes. It's worth considering, because there might be a sudden dip in the exchange rate before you receive full payment, potentially leaving you out of pocket.

Today I do factor exchange rates into my design pricing, and, given that I'm based in the United Kingdom, I keep the British pound as my consistent monetary figure. In every quote, I show both the client's local currency and the pound figure alongside it, stating that my pricing is based on the strength of the pound at the time of the initial quote. Including the client's local currency saves her from having to perform the conversion herself. I determine exchange rates using the currency converter on xe.com, which provides real-time updates of rate changes.

But what happens when the rate dips? Say, for example, that I'm working with a client in Japan, and the British pound becomes weaker against the Japanese yen during the course of the project. While it might be tempting to try and revisit the fee with my client, it's important to keep in mind that I have already agreed upon a set fee for the work. In these cases, I need to take whatever loss occurs on the chin. Not only do I risk disappointing the client, but I also wouldn't consider lowering my fee if things swung the other way and the value of the yen dropped dramatically.

You could always factor fluctuations into your initial client agreement, but it's something I choose not to do. The important part is getting paid in the currency I use to pay my overhead, because then I know that my expenditures are covered, regardless of the exchange rates.

Spec work

I often hear from young designers who are tempted to take part in logo design contests so that they can earn some money. They ask if it's a good way to break into the design profession and build their portfolios.

The reality is that only one party will benefit from design contests, and that's the owner of the website hosting them. Online logo design contests are spec work—and by spec work I mean giving away your intellectual property in the mere hope of getting paid. Designers have just as much of a right to get paid as any other professional, so don't believe the hype that these contest website owners push. They aim to make a profit by persuading you to give your work away for free. By doing so, you devalue the time and effort you have spent in getting where you are.

You might think that clients who host contests get value for money, but what they are presented with is a collection of designs made within minutes, with little to no regard for the goals, history, or competition of their business. There's a slim chance the client might see a design that appeals to her tastes, but will it appeal to the tastes of her company's audience? That's what you are paid to research.

Entering contests is not a good way to build a portfolio, either. It's unlikely that you will receive any feedback on your designs, and when you do, it will almost certainly be from someone unqualified to give constructive advice.

If you're truly interested in learning how to improve your design skills, look for feedback from designers with experience. One option is to enroll in a respected design course in which you will be taught from those qualified to teach, and where you will learn how to handle constructive criticism—a vital part of dealing with clients.

Another idea is to join an online design forum where you can receive feedback on the work you post. HOWDesign.com is one forum I used to visit regularly. It proved a great help in my earlier years of study, and the forum members included many talented designers who offered advice.

But perhaps you already have a solid portfolio and see logo design contests as a chance to work on real-world projects. In this case, instead try contacting local nonprofit organizations and offer to work pro bono (in other words, donate your work for the public good). There are multiple benefits to this type of work over the contest approach: You'll deal firsthand with your client the whole way through the project, which is ideal for building confidence; you'll build local business contacts, which can help attract future clients; and you'll be much more likely to actually see your designs in use, which is great for your portfolio.

Everyone makes mistakes

Making mistakes is an important part of the pricing process. Every designer makes them at one point or another, and you will never truly know if you're pricing your services accordingly until you make a mistake. Here's a case in point. A couple of years into my entrepreneurial adventure, I was approached by a potential client who would have been my biggest client at that point in my career.

After I gained an understanding of the firm's design needs, we came to an agreement on price. Midway through the project, my contact asked me to supply design work that was outside of the original agreement. So I sent a new quote. But my contact also let me in on a secret: What I was charging was well below what the company typically paid for a similar service. In fact, it was so far below what was expected that my client almost hired another agency.

This was a good lesson for me. I learned that clients expect to pay a premium for a premium quality service, and by charging a lower rate, you give the impression that your service is of lower quality. So be very cautious about underselling yourself. And remember that once you set a price, it's very difficult to negotiate it upward later in the process.

As much as we loathe them at the time, mistakes can be incredibly helpful in the long term, but only if you learn from them.

Chapter seven

From pencil to PDF

To be a good designer, you must be curious about life; the strongest ideas are born from the experiences we have and the knowledge we gain from them. The more we see and the more we know, the more ammunition we can stockpile for generating ideas.

I'm frequently asked how to integrate this stockpile into actual logo concepts, and that's what we're going to focus on in this chapter. We'll look at the two vital steps in this process—mind-mapping and sketching—and then talk about what to include when preparing your presentation PDFs for the client.

Mind-mapping

Using mind maps helps you consider as many different design directions as possible, and at the stage when they're most needed. It's a relatively straightforward process of word association. You write a word that's central to the design brief, and then branch out from it, writing other words that spring to mind. These additional words could come after some thought, or after researching the central topic. The idea is to form as large a "thought cloud" as possible, giving you a strong tool to refer to when it comes to the next stage—sketching.

Mind-mapping is particularly useful in the design profession because it's very effective for working through these important steps of the design process:

- Collecting your thoughts
- Generating ideas
- Getting into a creative groove
- Associating words with images

I've been using mind maps for as long as I've been studying design. It's a tried and tested formula, and other designers often ask me to provide more detail on the intricacies of this practice. So let's take a look at one or two of them.

**Komplett Fitness
mind map**

By David Airey

2008

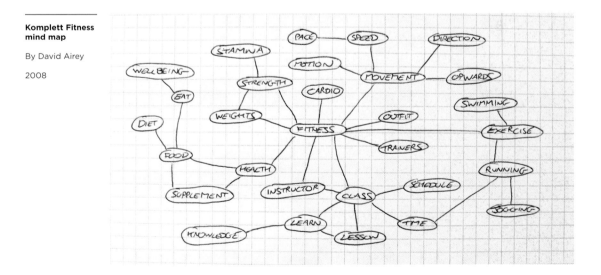

**Meadows
Renewable
mind map**

By David Airey

2008

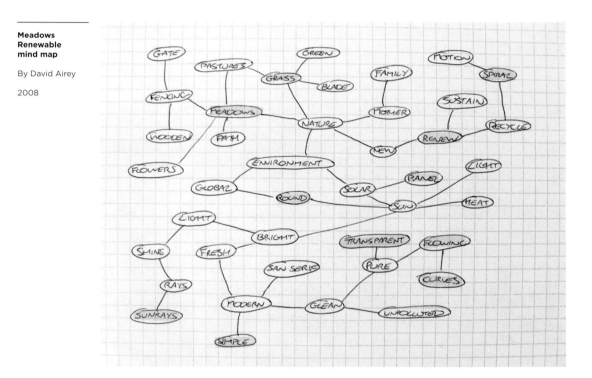

I generated the mind map above for Meadows Renewable, a Las Vegas-based energy company that sells solar panel systems, solar water heaters, solar attic fans, and various other renewable and sustainable energy products.

Notice the highlighting. If I map a word I think will adapt well to the sketching process, I usually mark it with a highlighter. This helps me focus on the stronger ideas.

**Ecometrica
mind map**

By David Airey

2008

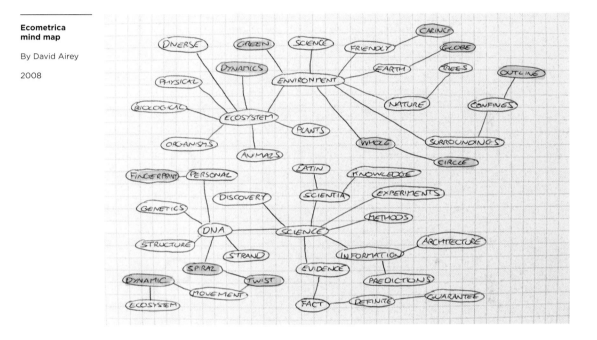

I was assigned in 2008 to create a brand identity for the
Scottish firm Ecometrica, which conducts science-based
analyses of the impact of climate and ecosystem changes.
I began my mind map by focusing on two words, "environment"
and "science." I placed each word in a separate "bubble" and
then made a note of all the words I could associate with each
one, which helped move my imagination in directions I might
not have gone otherwise.

Relating these words into actual shapes and symbols is easier than it looks. For instance, from my "science bubble" came an association with "DNA," and from DNA came an association with "personal," and from personal came an association with "fingerprint." Basing Ecometrica's logomark on a fingerprint became one of my central concept possibilities.

**Ecometrica
mind map**

By David Airey

2008

**Daily Nest
mind map
(opposite)**

By David Airey

2008

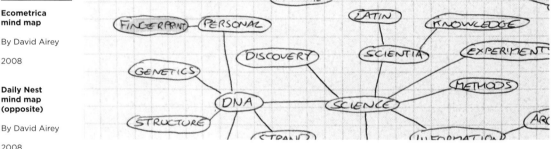

I usually spend at least two days of a project mapping word associations. I find that the two-day allotment provides me at least one night to sleep on my ideas, which really helps. Gaining some distance from the project at night is productive, as is a rested mind in the morning.

Once you have a thorough map on paper, you can use it as the cornerstone of the next step.

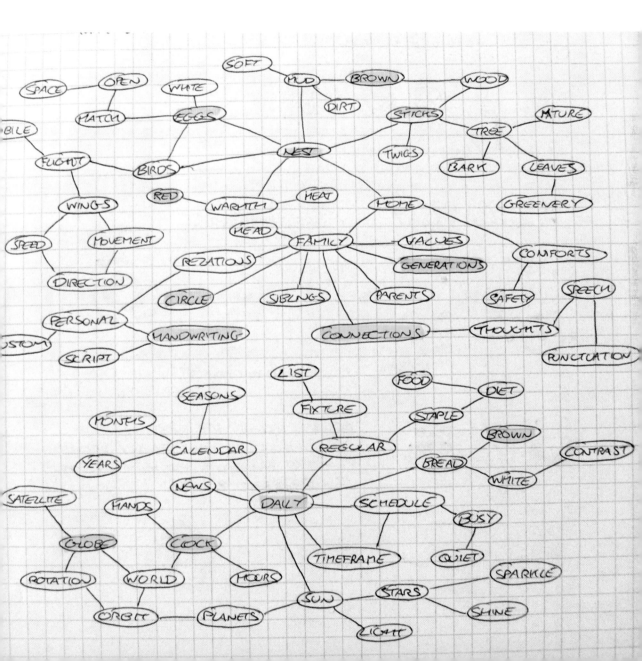

The fundamental necessity of the sketchpad

A by-product of sub-par design courses is that aspiring designers today see computers as the only truly necessary tool. On the contrary. By removing the computer from the creative process, you gain much more freedom when translating your thoughts.

You learned to draw before you learned how to use a computer. Why? Because it's easier. It's less restricting. And it's more creative. You want a circle here? A stroke there? No problem. Just do it. Translating the same process to a computer requires unnecessary steps that hinder your creative flow.

Ecometrica sketches

By David Airey

2008

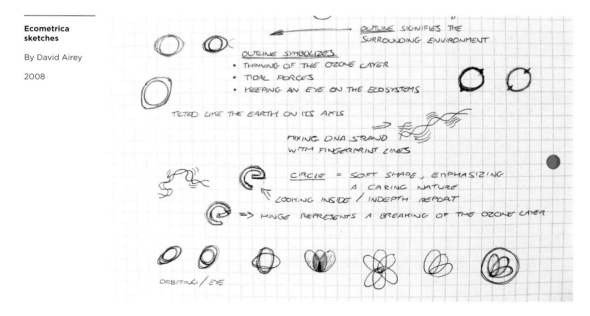

The sketchpad is a conceptual playground—a tangible scene where an idea can be batted around and subjected to the immediacy of uncensored thoughts. Random concepts collide with intention. Suggestions are made. Some stick. Others are tossed. Eventually your concept develops structure, and only then are you ready to use a computer.

It's vital to keep an open mind and not limit yourself during the sketching process. Even if your ideas seem too far-fetched, it's best to make a visual note of all the thoughts that cross your mind.

Remember, too, that your drawing skills aren't important. What is important is that you churn out as many ideas as possible before turning to your computer. Your mind map gives you access to the most important thoughts you can associate with the company you've been hired to represent. Sketch based on a single thought. Merge two together. Combine a group. There should be a huge array of possibilities. Whatever comes into your head, sketch it before it's gone.

Let's look at some examples in which the use of a pencil has led to effective results.

The Tenth Commandment

Designer Nancy Wu was given the task of creating a logo for Tenth Avenue Alliance Church in Vancouver, British Columbia (popularly known as just "Tenth Church"). The clever result was born from these sketches.

Nancy Wu's preliminary sketching for Tenth Church

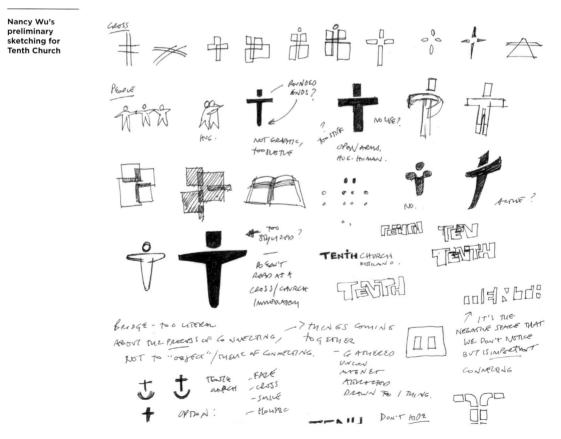

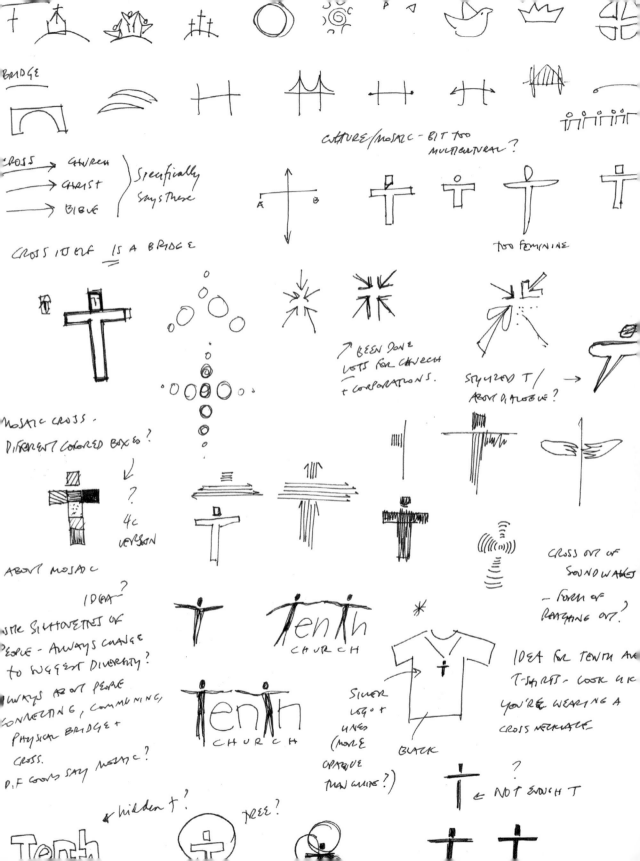

BRIDGE

CROSS → CHURCH
→ CHRIST   } Specifically
→ BIBLE   } says these

CROSS ITSELF IS A BRIDGE

CULTURE/MOSAIC - BIT TOO
MULTICULTURAL?

A   B

TOO FEMININE

MOSAIC CROSS.
DIFFERENT COLORED BOXES?

?
4c
VERSION

BEEN DONE
LOTS FOR CHURCH
+ CORPORATIONS.

STYLIZED T/
ABOUT DIALOGUE?

ABOUT MOSAIC

IDEA?
USE SILHOUETTES OF
PEOPLE - ALWAYS CHANGE
TO SUGGEST DIVERSITY?
ALWAYS ABOUT PEOPLE
CONNECTING, COMMUNING,
PHYSICAL BRIDGE +
CROSS.
D.F GOULD SAY MOSAIC?

CROSS OUT OF
SOUND WAVES
- FORM OF
REACHING OUT?

Tenth
CHURCH

Tenth
CHURCH

SILVER
LOGO +
LINES
(MORE
OPAQUE
THAN WHITE?)

BLACK

IDEA FOR TENTH AVE
T-SHIRTS - LOOK LIK
YOU'RE WEARING A
CROSS NECKLACE

?
← NOT ENOUGH T

hidden t?

TREE?

Tenth

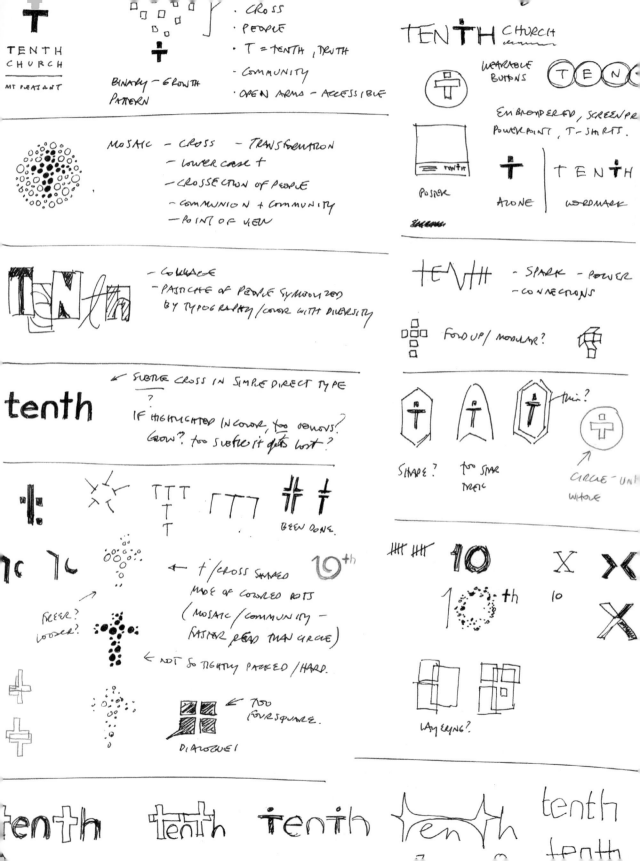

TENTH
CHURCH
MT PLEASANT

BINARY - GROWTH
PATTERN

- CROSS
- PEOPLE
- T = TENTH, TRUTH
- COMMUNITY
- OPEN ARMS - ACCESSIBLE

TENTH CHURCH

WEARABLE BUTTONS

TEN

EMBROIDERED, SCREENPR
POWERPOINT, T-SHIRTS.

POSTER

ALONE | **tenth**
WORDMARK

MOSAIC - CROSS - TRANSFORMATION
- LOWER CASE +
- CROSS SECTION OF PEOPLE
- COMMUNION + COMMUNITY
- POINT OF VIEW

- COLLAGE
- PASTICHE OF PEOPLE SYMBOLIZED
BY TYPOGRAPHY/COLOR WITH DIVERSITY

- SPARK - POWER
- CONNECTIONS

FOLD UP/MODULAR?

tenth

← SUBTLE CROSS IN SIMPLE DIRECT TYPE
?
IF HIGHLIGHTED IN COLOR, TOO OBVIOUS?
GROW?. TOO SUBTLE IT GETS LOST ?

SHAPE?   TOO STAR
          TREK

thin?

CIRCLE - UN
WHOLE

BEEN DONE.

FREER?
LOOSER?

← +/CROSS SHAPED
MADE OF COLORED DOTS
(MOSAIC/COMMUNITY -
FASTER READ THAN CIRCLE)

10th

10th

X   X

10

← NOT SO TIGHTLY PACKED/HARD.

← TOO
FOURSQUARE.

DIALOGUE?

LAYERING?

tenth   **tenth**   **tenth**   **tenth**

tenth

Church officials wanted a refreshed brand identity that avoided stylistic trends, clichés, and traditional cues that speak of the past, versus what the church is accomplishing today. They wanted the design to represent human emotion and vitality, and reflect the virtues of being down-to-earth, welcoming, and authentic.

Tenth Church

By Nancy Wu

2009

TENTH

At first glance, the logo is deceptively simple. But a lot of behind-the-scenes effort goes into every successful identity project.

"The effectiveness as a mark was apparent on launch day, in watching how church members and visitors reacted to it," said Wu. "It was accessible, and people seemed to understand it instinctively."

The simple wordmark incorporates a graphic icon with multiple conceptual themes of worship, welcome, transformation, outreach, and the cross.

Pinning the map

Canada-based designer Josiah Jost, of Siah Design, created this logo for Filmaps.com—a website for people to share and discover filmmaking locations. The goal for the logo was to create an icon that could communicate just that, and Josiah understood the value of the sketching process.

Filmaps

By Josiah Jost of
Siah Design

2009

"I sketched several concepts, which provided many options for combining elements from filmmaking and map locations in a creative way," said Josiah.

Filmaps executives and Josiah liked the pushpin idea, since pushpins are often associated with both marking a spot on a map and the filmstrip.

Filmaps sketches

By Josiah Jost of
Siah Design

2009

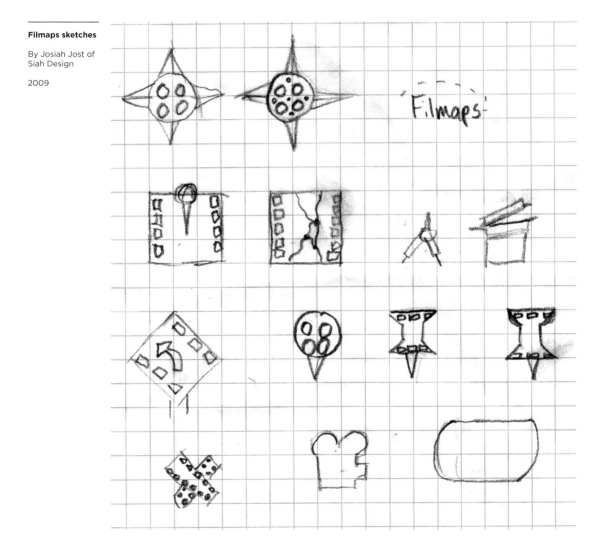

Internationally recognized

La Internacional, an independent drugstore in San Francisco, specializes in natural medicine products. Well aware that its name didn't begin to describe the type or range of products and services available, the management asked studio1500, a California-based graphic design firm, to create a mark that clearly communicated the store's focus on natural medicine.

Here are some of the sketches that studio1500 Partner and Creative Director Julio Martínez produced.

La Internacional sketches

By studio1500

Partner and creative director: Julio Martínez

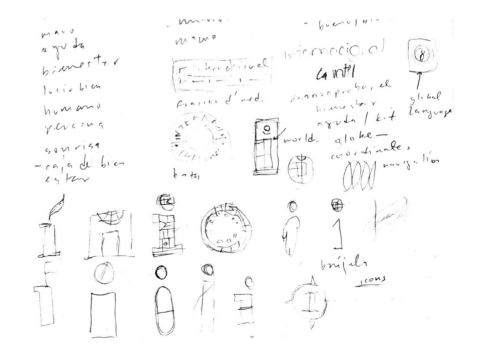

**La Internacional
sketches**

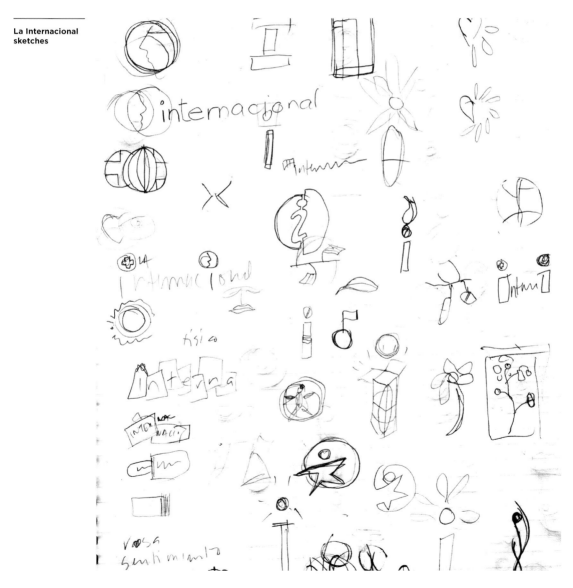

These are the three logos that studio1500 presented in digital form. The client selected the design at the top. The incorporation of a pill in the design clearly suggests "drugstore," and the green circle emphasizes the natural aspect of the products La Internacional sells.

La Internacional

By studio1500

2008

Keep in mind that a logo doesn't have to reflect in a literal way what the business is about. But when it does, and especially when it manages to do it without hitting you over the head with the idea, it really can be a winner.

No set time

The first idea you sketch for a client is unlikely to be the one that gets chosen. But sometimes, when your creative energy is really flowing and you completely "get" your client, it ends up that way.

studio1500's Martínez produced this logo within minutes of sitting down at the drawing table for Elemental8, an industrial design studio located in San Jose, California.

Elemental8

By studio1500

Partner and creative director: Julio Martínez

2008

**Elemental8
sketches**

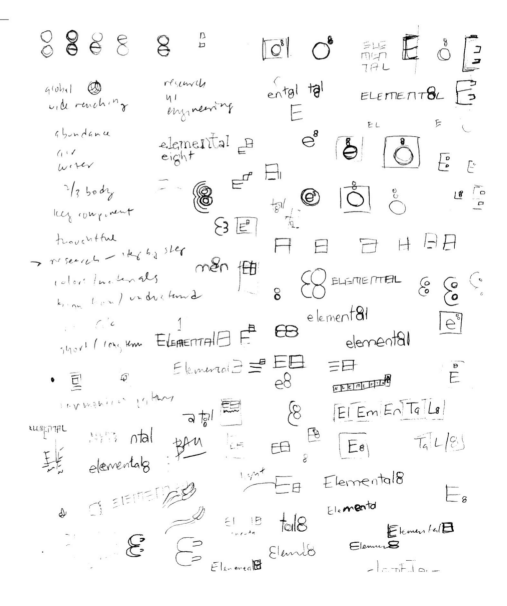

The idea represented two open circles hovering near each other, as if suspended in air.

"It was very clearly an 8, but one that left its components intact as whole circles," said Martínez. "The openness and precision it evoked resonated with the team, but it also worked on another level: The studio was founded by two partners, so the mark alluded to that fact by depicting two separate elements joining forces to create a unified whole."

Think about the words that would've appeared in a mind map for this client. "Eight" is one of the most obvious. And "two," for the studio's two partners. Put those words together with a little sketching, and when you've created two circles, one above the other, it hardly comes across as rocket science. And it's not. When you break it down, the identity design process is relatively straightforward, albeit constructed by a number of small steps, each playing an important role.

Dress for success

Once you feel like you have several strong design possibilities, you'll want to render them as presentational PDFs. You should always document your work in a PDF file, even if your presentation is in person. PDFs are helpful because the layout and formatting of the content is fixed—that is, it won't change, regardless of the software your client uses to view it.

Because half the battle of creating an effective design lies in pleasing your client, make sure you render only your best ideas. Don't include any designs you think might be unsuitable, or you risk diluting the quality of your great designs with sub-par possibilities. Including ideas that you're not sure of also introduces the possibility that your client will choose the weaker candidate among a group of otherwise great options. Remember Murphy's Law!

Circle sketches

By David Airey

2005

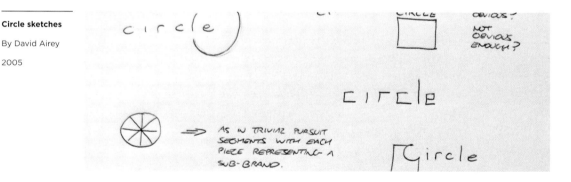

One of my very first clients was a web-hosting company in South Africa called Circle. It was up to me to create the company's logo, but in my eagerness to please, I presented all of my ideas for feedback. Had I known that by doing so I'd overwhelm the client, making it impossible to choose one idea out of so many possibilities, I would have limited the presentation to the ideas that I was convinced would work.

A few bad apples spoil the barrel. The project stalled and was never completed.

Black and white before color

Now let's look at an example in which only the best ideas were presented, and with great skill and foresight.

160over90, a design agency in Philadelphia, was given the task of rebranding the Woodmere Art Museum, which houses what it calls a "rich, three-centuries-and-counting legacy that includes American art from before we officially became America."

Like any good agency, designers first worked up a series of sketches before presenting the three strongest logos to Woodmere—the monogram, the signature, and the perspective. The agency's standard practice is to initially present designs only in black and white, since its designers have found that color biases a client's ability to focus on the form and ideas that the logo communicates.

Woodmere's monogram concept

By 160over90

2008

**Woodmere's
signature
concept**

**Woodmere's
perspective
concept**

Woodmere chose an evolved variation of the monogram option, with its simple graphic shapes that emphasize dimension and connection. With this design, 160over90 created solid graphic forms that feel classical but turn into pieces of modern identity architecture that can also become patterns and hold imagery. Once the client was firmly leaning toward using the monogram, agency designers rendered it in color, and provided a nice touch by showing the final colors as Pantone swatches.

Woodmere Art Museum

Chosen design with Pantone swatches

By 160over90

2008

Woodmere**ArtMuseum**

Woodmere**ArtMuseum**

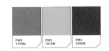

Leaving color options for the end of the process is a great idea because it's a detail that can be easily changed. And the last thing you want is for your client to be turned off by an effective idea simply because he doesn't like the color scheme.

Where Photoshop comes into play

Showing your designs in context—in other words, as they will be seen by others—is key to helping your client visualize how great you can make the company look. It's comparable to buying a car. The car might show a fresh paint job and have that "new car smell," but unless you take it for a test drive, you won't be entirely convinced. That's why showing your logo designs in context can be what finally cements the deal with your client.

Using Photoshop to add your logo concepts to photos of cars, building signage, billboard space, business card mockups, and so on, you can augment the PDFs of your best ideas for your presentation to the client. The more variety you create, the more consistent the usage becomes, and the more attractive the outcome will appear.

**Kerling mockups
in Photoshop**

By
Andrew Sabatier

Brand
consultancy:
Karakter, now
Siegel+Gale

2007

London-based designer Andrew Sabatier effectively used Photoshop to create digitized mockups for his client Kerling, a major Nordic supplier of vinyl chloride.

Kerling

Designer:
Andrew Sabatier

Kerling is a vinyl chloride company on a mission to make the world a better place. We are the leading thinkers in sustainable polymer production. You can think of our plastics as plastic with a conscience

Most clients won't have time to concern themselves with every step in the design process. They'll be focused on the end result, so the more tangible your concepts appear, the more the client will be able to visualize the benefits.

As much as we like to think otherwise, books are judged by their covers, so make sure your identity presentations—the PDFs and mockups done in Photoshop—look professional.

Make sure, too, that you save your PDF files with the date in the actual filename, since there might be some back-and-forth with your client. Seeing the date in the filename helps with version control and ensures you and your client are looking at the same document when talking things through on the phone.

The pen is mightier than the mouse

We've looked at what happens up to the point of the initial client presentation. You've put a lot of hard work into mind-mapping, sketching your ideas, and presenting only the best options to the client. The PDF is in your client's hands, and you're awaiting feedback.

Let's recap the main points of this chapter:

- Mind-mapping helps you consider as many different design directions as possible.
- Even the most simplistic designs are helped by an extensive sketching session.
- A pen or pencil offers much more control and creative freedom than a computer mouse, so don't use a computer until your ideas are in place.
- Don't fret if you think you can't draw, because what's important is that you document your ideas so that you can either build upon them or rule them out.
- Don't be tempted to show a client all of your sketches, because there will undoubtedly be directions you don't want to pursue, and it would be most unfortunate if the client chose one of those directions.
- Make sure your PDFs help the client focus on the idea, and not on an easily changed aspect like color.
- As much as we like to think otherwise, books are judged by their covers, so make sure your identity presentations look professional to keep clients on board.

At this stage of the process, you might consider the job nearly complete, but don't forget you still need to present your ideas to the client. That's where we're headed next.

Chapter eight

The art of the conversation

You've met with your client and gathered information. You've conducted thorough research, spent hours sketching, and worked on digitized versions of your strongest concepts. Now you're ready to make that client presentation—a stage of the process that can cause undue pressure and anxiety.

If you're one of many designers who finds presentations a bit daunting and unpredictable, one of the ways that you can alleviate the pressure is to try and look at client presentations from a different angle. Delivering your ideas shouldn't foster the worry associated with a "big reveal." At the same time, this stage of the process is about way more than simply showing a few pictures and asking, "So, what do you reckon?"

Presentations are really nothing more than a conversation with your client. If you've fostered that conversation throughout the design process—by listening to your client and responding thoughtfully, by clearly articulating how the process works, and by maintaining the dialogue with the decision-makers in the organization—then the presentation itself is just a continuation of that ongoing conversation.

But presentations are also about the art of delicate negotiation, just as much as they are about the designs you've generated. You need to be clear and concise with your explanations. You need to know how to persuade your client that your design (or one of them) is the best possible visual representation for his company. You must also know how to edit your thoughts so that everything you say has a valid reason for being said.

This chapter examines the critical elements for successful conversations, as well as some of the conditions that are often inherent in unsuccessful ones. When you're finished reading it, you should have some sense of what presentation strategies you can use to get your clients to fully embrace at least some of your design ideas.

Deal with the decision-maker

In Chapter 4, I touched on how important it is to make sure you deal with the decision-maker during at least some phases of a project. Moving forward, I'll be referring to the decision-maker as the "committee," since the clients you want to attract will probably have more than one person involved in choosing a visual identity.

Working directly with the committee for the duration of the project isn't always possible—most likely you will have been working with a single point of contact (perhaps a brand manager as opposed to a CEO or board of directors) at least some of the time up until this point. But when it comes time to deliver your design ideas, dealing with the committee is critical. The last thing you want is for your carefully crafted explanations to devolve into a game of "phone tag," in which rationales are conveyed and usually quickly distorted through a mediator.

Uh oh, you say, not the notorious "design by committee"! I know, I know, some of the worst work in the world has resulted from committee reviews. If one individual opts for a certain element of one design, while others like different details of other designs, it's easy to end up with a completely different design from the ones you worked so hard to produce.

However, if you are in control of the committee review process, you can use the strengths of each participant to iron out any kinks in your strongest concepts, and ultimately produce an iconic identity design that both you and the committee as a whole are delighted by.

Back in 2008, I was working on a brand identity project for Tokyo-based Berthier Associates, an interior design firm with clients such as Air France and Ferrari. Throughout the process I had the ideal point of contact—managing director Dominique Berthier—but because of who he was, I wrongly assumed there would be no committee involvement. After all, I was dealing with the man who had the final say over the outcome. But did I ask? No. I assumed. And we all know where that leads.

Berthier had his own team of designers (or committee) at his disposal. Granted, they weren't graphic designers per se—they were interior designers. But the elements we graphic designers use, such as line, space, texture, color, tone, and form, can be carried through all design professions. So there's a definite overlap in what we do.

**Berthier website
screenshots**

Logo by
David Airey

2008

In hindsight, it was obvious Berthier would want committee approval before the project was completed. This desire, and my inability at the time to anticipate it or ask about it, meant the design process would be significantly lengthened as a result of internal committee meetings.

But such committee involvement also meant I could draw upon the design strengths of Berthier's team to produce the strongest visual identity possible. Ultimately, the committee proved to be a great asset throughout our working relationship.

Since that time, I have always made a point of asking my contact for every project, "Who will have input about the design directions I present?" Had I known to do this with the Berthier project from the outset, I would've realized I needed to increase the project time frame to accommodate the internal meetings, which would have gone a long way in keeping deadline expectations in check.

Ensuring you get to present your ideas to the committee rather than to your point of contact doesn't happen overnight. It's an ongoing process—a series of steps or rules you must adhere to from the very beginning of the project to make sure that when the time comes, you get to present your ideas directly to the people who will be making decisions about them.

Blair Enns, founder of Win Without Pitching, a consulting firm initiated to help agencies deal with their clients, believes that designers can actually improve the quality of their work and avoid all the traps of "design by committee" by adhering to four basic rules:

- Conspire with your point of contact
- Avoid intermediation
- Take control
- Keep the committee involved

Enns is a speaker, author, and teacher who has worked with design firms, advertising agencies, and public relations agencies around the world to help them migrate away from high cost, low integrity, pitch-based business strategies. Instead he advocates for a model in which the agency commands the high ground in the relationship and shapes how its services are bought and sold. I've found that his advice has helped me create smoother, more effective relationships with my clients.

All this might sound a little cryptic, so the next few sections of this chapter delve into the details of these four rules, with a few anecdotes of my own.

Rule #1: Conspire to help

An introduction to any client usually begins with a single point of contact. You could be dealing with a nonprofit organization, in which the committee is often a board. In this case, your contact might be an employee. Or maybe your client is an architectural studio, with the committee comprising the partners in the firm. Your contact might be an office manager or marketing assistant who is not a partner or even an architect.

According to Enns, this contact will most likely be just as frustrated as you are about the potential pitfalls of committee-based decision-making. In these cases, empathy is a powerful marketing tool.

By placing yourself in your contact's shoes, you will likely see that presenting the design ideas to the committee as a whole is at the top of her priority list, too, and that any help you can offer will be greatly appreciated.

I was tasked in 2006 with creating a logo and stationery package for a company in Scotland called Davidson Locksmith. From the start of the project until it was time to present my ideas, I dealt with Paul Davidson, the company owner's son.

During the beginning stages of the project, I asked him who would be involved in signing off on the design. Davidson told me his father would have final say. So I proceeded to explain that I had a lot of experience in presenting design ideas, and that I wanted to help by presenting to both of them simultaneously when the time came. The project was a great success, in no small measure because I was able to work directly with both decision-makers at presentation time.

Davidson
Locksmith

By David Airey

2006

From the beginning, you should make it very clear you're there to help, and that you're well-versed in helping people like your contact achieve approval from the committee. Together, the two of you can conspire to ultimately win the confidence of the committee.

Rule #2: Avoid intermediation

The first rule—conspire to help—is also part of the second rule: avoid intermediation at all costs at presentation time.

Think about it. You may have been hired as an expert, but if your designs are presented by your contact—a subordinate of the committee—they could be perceived with lesser value. And what if there are objections to your design decisions? How effectively can these be addressed by your contact?

You also have no idea what your contact's relationship might be with the committee or whether any personal issues exist that could interfere with the committee's acceptance of your ideas. "Office politics" might exist within the committee itself that interfere with committee members' acceptance of your designs—issues that your contact is powerless to subdue.

When you think about it, having someone else explain your design decisions places an unnecessary barrier between you and the decision-maker. You need to remove anything that can hinder the process at this very delicate stage.

But sometimes this is easier said than done. One identity design project I worked on early in my career was particularly challenging in this respect. My client was located in Greece, and my point of contact was one of two partners, with both partners having an equal say over the final design decision.

The issue was that while my point of contact spoke fluent English, the other partner did not. I knew this meant the explanation for my design decisions held the potential to be lost in translation, with my point of contact acting as mediator, but I wasn't sure how to work around it. I ended up presenting to my point of contact, and at a later time, which in some instances was a few days later, he presented to his partner. Not only was the translation a potential hindrance, but the delay between presentations led to vital reasoning being ommitted or forgotten.

At the time, I wasn't aware how damaging this could be to the design outcome. As it turned out, my client rejected all four of my initial concepts in favor of a much more generic solution that the partners had created between them. Neither partner had any design experience, and as much as I tried to persuade them against their choice, it was too late. I had already lost control of the process.

Even when all the decision-makers speak your language, getting your point of contact to agree that you are the only one who can present your ideas to the committee can sometimes be a challenge. That's where Rule #1 comes into play. You've already positioned yourself as someone who's there to help—someone who can aid in the task of gaining committee approval. To further your cause, you might also offer to deliver a dry run of your presentation to your contact before the committee gets a chance to see it, so that your contact is more comfortable about your intentions.

Enns recommends that if all else fails when trying to convince your contact, use the phrase "agency policy." Tell her that it's your agency's policy: Designers with your firm must be the ones to present design concepts to decision-makers.

"You'll be surprised how often resistance melts away when they hear these words," said Enns.

Rule #3: Take control

Once you've attained the goal of meeting with the committee, what's critical is that you control the meeting from the very beginning. Keeping a tight reign on proceedings will help immeasurably in securing approval for your design concepts.

But before you unveil your designs, it's worth remembering that months could have passed since the committee discussed the details of the design brief. CEOs, directors, and business owners all have a lot of other concerns, so by jogging their memories, you'll ensure that everyone's in tune with why time and money are being spent on brand identity.

Briefly state the project background—why a new or refined identity is needed, what the goals for a new design are, and how having a new identity will actually help the company turn a profit. You can judge the depth of detail you should go into by the amount of time that has passed since the briefing stage.

The more time that has passed, the more detail you'll want to provide. But don't go overboard. It's just a refresher, not an essay, and your audience is comprised of very busy people. A couple of minutes talking should suffice.

As clear as you think your ideas are, you might find a little design jargon slip into your language here and there. This can quickly lose your client's train of thought, so remember, you're not talking to another designer. Make your points clearly, without jargon, and keep them related to the original design brief.

Outline the ground rules
Once you've brought everyone up to speed, you want to maintain control of the presentation by outlining a few ground rules.

Committee members will often see the showcasing of design ideas as an invitation to make their own design decisions. It's your task to remind the committee that while their input is critical, they should resist the temptation to jump into the design fray themselves. You're the expert, and if the discussion devolves into them telling you what colors or fonts to use, the brand will inevitably be weakened.

Let them know that what you need from them is strategic input and executional freedom. Something like, "So let me know if you think the creative isn't meeting our agreed-upon strategy, but refrain from trying to figure out and suggest how to fix it. That's what you're paying me to do."

You might even provide the committee a few examples, like "Say you think a blue is too weak for an organization trying to present an image of strength. Or say you think the typeface is too old-fashioned. Voicing those impressions is critical to the success of a project. But refrain from saying 'Make the blue darker' or 'Why don't you try Arugula Modern?' You have to trust that I can find the right design solution based on your feedback. Otherwise, we risk diluting the strength of the brand identity because I'm listening to the design ideas of too many non-designers."

You might also find that many committees contain one strong personality within the group—a person who holds more influence than the others simply because he is more outspoken. This can create awkward dynamics and undesirable outcomes. However, as an outsider merely enforcing protocol, you have the ability to bring balance back to the committee when insiders could not. Do not underestimate the value of this outside facilitation! Take control and hold your ground.

Don't wait until the presentation

Of course, if you haven't maintained some level of control from the very beginning of the entire process—way before the presentation—you likely will have a difficult time maintaining control at this point. The relationship you have with your client throughout the process is vitally important for the acceptance of your ideas.

"Early in your first interaction with the committee you have the choice of establishing the relationship as either one of patient (client) and practitioner (agency) or one of customer and order-taker," said Enns. "You will be viewed as a doctor or a waiter, depending on the degree to which you take control of the situation."

He's right. It's an easy trap to fall into—finding yourself as an order-taker—and during my earliest projects it happened far too often. The client would tell me to use this typeface, or that color, and I'd say, "No problem. Expect to receive the changes by tomorrow." In such instances the client is doing your job, only without the benefit of your design education and experience. This is hardly helpful when creating iconic brand identities.

If I'd have known the tips detailed in this chapter when I was starting out, I'm positive it would've saved me many a headache and a lot of continuous back-and-forth on the latest whim of my client's taste.

Rule #4: Keep the committee involved

There's an old saying, "Keep your friends close and your enemies closer." Whether you consider the committee a friend or foe, you can help to close the deal by defining the role of the committee in the client-agency relationship very early in the process. Part of this definition should make very clear at which points in the process input will be helpful, and when it will be counterproductive.

Knowing that the committee is indeed part of the process and that its feedback is vital to the project's success is highly reassuring to any client. The committee will be far easier to work with when it is included in development along the way—especially on the strategic issues that characterize the early part of the relationship—rather than apprised of it afterward. You just need to set the ground rules for how and when that feedback comes in.

I was hired in 2004 by a landscape gardening firm to create its first brand identity. For the first few weeks, and after a number of face-to-face meetings, the design process was running smoothly, but when it came time to present my ideas, things quickly turned sour.

What I didn't know was that even before I was hired, the committee already had a firm grasp of the design they wanted to see. They wanted me to bring it to life rather than create a visual representation from my own research and brainstorming. The only hitch is that they didn't inform me of this desire. Instead, they considered the possibility that I *might* create a design they liked even better and so decided to remain mum.

I strongly believed that the ideas I presented were more relevant to my client's audience, but the reality was the committee members had already attached themselves to their own original idea. So the month I spent on research, brainstorming, sketching, and conceptualizing was not important to them.

Had I been more thorough about setting the ground rules at the beginning of the project, I could've saved a month of misused time. I should have said something like, "With your help, I will create a number of possible design directions that are ideally suited to your potential customers. Once the different ideas have been presented, we can choose the most effective option and either move forward with it, or tweak it a little after your feedback."

Of course, I also should have asked in the initial meeting if my client had any preconceived design ideas. Regretfully, I didn't.

Your goal at each meeting is to attain approval and consensus among the committee. What you don't need is to have worked through a solid strategy for your final concepts only to hear concerns about the underlying message. Strategy is one of the first aspects you and the committee should have reached agreement on, and revisiting it at this late stage is extremely counterproductive.

Now that you know Enns' four rules for ensuring the presentation goes the way that you hope it will go, it's time to focus on the scheduling.

Don't forget to under-promise and then over-deliver

Maintaining accuracy in hitting your deadlines is key to a healthy client relationship. Think of the last time you purchased a product online. You wanted to know when to expect delivery, didn't you? Design clients are no different when it comes to revisions. They depend on you delivering when you say you will. So when you're unsure how long a task will take to complete, always give the client an estimate that is longer than the amount of time you're guessing it will take.

Why? Because unexpected setbacks can crop up at any time. Think of the computer you work on each day, the Adobe software you use on a regular basis, the Internet connection you pay for, the electricity that powers your office, and your good health.

All of these necessities are by no means guaranteed, and it almost goes without saying you'll have a computer problem at one time or another that will affect your productivity. Even if your equipment stays up and running, a human being can let you down. That's because even the most independent designer relies on others to get the job done.

When I was hired by Norwegian company Komplett Fitness in 2008, I knew I'd be moving home to Northern Ireland from Scotland one month into our working relationship. By letting my client know about the move at the start of the project, I was able to explain why the design process would take longer than normal. Think of what's involved when relocating: the installation of a new telephone line and the set-up of an Internet connection, as well as the time and stress involved in packing and unpacking all of my worldly belongings.

Komplett Fitness

By David Airey

2008

Because my client was aware of the extended time frame, he was happy to accommodate my personal needs.

So factor the worst into your delivery time frame, and then impress your client by delivering ahead of schedule when things go smoothly.

Swallow that pride

It's important to reiterate that the design process always includes more than one party. And where discussions of any kind take place, you should always be prepared to swallow your pride and listen to the feedback. Of course, you should also expect your client to stick to the ground rules laid out earlier in this chapter. If not, you may need to remind the committee of those rules now and then.

Clients often do make suggestions that you might initially disagree with. Here's a case in point: I produced two strong concepts for Berthier Associates—the interior design firm mentioned earlier in this chapter—and the committee thought my preferred option (opposite top) was too organic to represent the company's structured approach. In retrospect, I realize that their choice (opposite bottom) was much more suited to the firm. And, it looked great on their business cards.

Even when everything inside of you is saying "no" to your client's feedback, it always pays to listen well and keep an open mind.

**Berthier organic
identity concept**

By David Airey

2008

**Berthier's chosen
identity**

By David Airey

2008

berthier

In another example, when I contracted with Yellow Pages on the redesign of its "walking fingers" logo, I was tasked with retaining the fingers in the design, but presenting them in a different way from before.

Some members of the committee were convinced that adding a dart alongside the fingers would improve the design. (Yellow Pages was using a dart as a symbol on its website at the time). I was certain it would not.

The committee was not aware of the "focus on one thing" concept that I discuss in Chapter 3, so I realized that committee members needed to see for themselves that adding the dart would infuse the design with too many elements.

Rather than getting defensive, I delivered on the request. But I also coupled the idea with another that I believed was an even better improvement, and explained why when I presented it.

Once the results were compared, it was easier for the committee to deem its design idea unsuitable. Clients are much less likely to resist your ideas moving forward if they've seen a graphic representation of how their own strategic interpretation pans out.

**Yellow Pages
dart concept**

By David Airey

2008

**Yellow Pages
alternative
concept**

By David Airey

2008

Remember during your presentation that what you're selling at this stage is the idea behind your best designs. Remind your client as often as necessary to focus on just the idea—the story behind the design concept—not the intricacies of the mark, or the particular choice of typeface. These lesser details can be ironed out when a single direction has been agreed upon. Otherwise, you could end up supplying revisions for more than one direction, which is an unnecessary cost for both parties.

Keep in mind, however, that things won't always go your way. Throughout my years of self-employment, I've presented brand identity projects to around 60 or 70 different clients. Two or three of my earliest presentations were so unsuccessful that they caused a stalemate in the process, and both my client and I lost out. Yet I've learned just as much, if not more, about the client relationship from those debacles as I have from the more successful ones.

Part III

Keep the fires burning

Chapter nine

Staying motivated

Design inspiration is a bit of a cliché. I'm asked time and again where I find the inspiration to do my job, or how I stay inspired, but it's important to remember that what we do, as designers, doesn't need inspiration in the true sense of the word. The ability to successfully complete the identity design process comes from the result of years of study, practice, and experience, as well as following a clearly defined set of steps— steps that have been detailed in the preceeding chapters.

However, motivation, not inspiration, can sometimes be an issue. You'd be naive to think that at some point during a long career in design, your motivation won't wane. A seemingly never-ending project; overly harsh criticism from your peers; the discovery that, after weeks of work, your favorite design concept has already been created by someone else for a different company; or simply being stuck at your computer for hours on end every day—all or any one of these factors can suck the motivation right out of you.

This chapter provides a range of motivational tips—some from me, and some from other designers—on how to keep your spirits up and the creative juices flowing during tough projects.

Never stop learning

You will never know all there is to know about design.

Our profession is constantly evolving, so to stay in the game you need to evolve with it. To get a sense of where our industry is headed, you need to look at where it's been. There's an incredible amount we can learn from the great iconic designers that came before us: people like Paul Rand (IBM logo), Paula Scher (Citi logo), and Tom Geismar (Mobil Oil logo). Those who have worked through a lifetime of design have amassed an incredible amount of experience, and I never tire of listening to their stories and anecdotes.

New-York-based Ivan Chermayeff has this to say about design: "To be effective over a reasonably long lifetime, all identities must be simple and appropriate. However, if they are not original or in any way provocative, thought-provoking, and noticeable, they will not accomplish their task."

Showtime

By
Ivan Chermayeff,
Chermayeff &
Geismar

1997

When you think about it, our peers are our biggest sources of motivation. There are few things in design that I enjoy more than seeing and reflecting upon the identity work of other designers. It pushes me to improve, and the most talented designers are those who have an interest in everything. I've already mentioned that you need to keep actively learning about the world, our history, and how we live our lives. You'll find a list of many iconic designers in the resources section at the back of the book, which you can use to further your knowledge of iconic design.

HarperCollins

By
Ivan Chermayeff,
Chermayeff &
Geismar

1990

I asked Belfast-based designer Richard Weston of design blog Ace Jet 170 what keeps him motivated. His answer very much supports this notion of always learning.

"The thing I always come back to is, 'Never think you know enough.' A thirst for knowledge and experience fuels my work and, to be honest, makes my working life a whole lot easier," said Weston.

"I've always had to deliver ideas and design work of a very high standard but, invariably, within a tight time frame and with an equally tight budget. I thrive under that kind of pressure but can only cope with it because I have made a point of learning and collecting loads of stuff. And it just keeps going. There's always something relevant and new to learn; whether it's about the disciplines we work within or the world at large. It's one of the main reasons why this is such a bloody brilliant job."

And a bloody brilliant job it is.

Be four years ahead

"I remember reading somewhere—and, sorry, I can't remember who said it—that a designer's tastes were seven years ahead of the general public," said David Hyde of studio hyde (aka davidthedesigner.com). "And that the art of being a successful designer was to be four years ahead. It's that elusive year four that still motivates me."

Create for you

"As a designer, I have found that I need to have creative experiences outside my client engagements, opportunities to create with no one to satisfy but myself," said Jerry Kuyper of Westport, Connecticut-based Jerry Kuyper Partners.

"This allows me to listen and collaborate with my clients more effectively. I also remind myself to go outside—the graphics are amazing."

Fusion

By Jerry Kuyper

Creative director:
Gene Seidman

2005

LodgeNet

By Jerry Kuyper

2008

Step away from the computer

As awe-inspiring as computers and the Internet are, they're still just tools we use to achieve our aim—creating iconic design. Our best achievements are born from our thoughts, and deftly interpreting the needs of our clients, neither of which have anything to do with the computer. Trying to brainstorm and generate ideas on the computer adds unnecessary friction to the design process.

"Although this is no longer the case, our business used to be made up of people who could draw," said designer Gerard Huerta. "This is how ideas were related to those who could not visualize. When you are stuck, walk away from the computer and draw. It will teach you how to see."

When you're fighting the urge to conceptualize design ideas at the computer, remember that design has been with us a lot longer than computers. Not just any design either, but design of a calibre to match or better what we can produce today.

So shut your computer down for at least the initial stages of the design process. Think things through. Grab that pen and pad you carry and start making notes and sketching ideas.

Balance your life

"Balance is the key," said California-based designer Lauren Krause of Creative Curio. "Balancing work-life, online-offline, digital-analog, personal-professional. Balance puts life into perspective, helps us to not lose our passion to bitterness, shows us inspiration through other experiences, and helps us maintain our sanity."

Journey back in time

I need only look at my earlier work to see the journey I've taken as a designer. You should try it, too. Dig out some of your earliest identity design projects and compare them to what you're working on today. I find it helps. Sometimes I cringe. But it helps, because I can see the progression.

Originn

By David Airey

2004

Henri Ehrhart

By David Airey

2009

HENRI EHRHART

VINS FINS D'ALSACE

Show relentless desire

"Every designer has a level of insecurity that can only be abated by the creative peer group respect or commercial success of their work," said Martin Lawless, creative director at London-based 300million. "Sadly, the warm, fuzzy, proud feeling of security doesn't last long. Sometimes, it's as short as the length of time it takes to make the winding walk back from the awards podium to the table of smiling workmates and your half-drunk client.

"Motivation comes from the relentless desire to get back to that briefest pause on the mountaintop. It's as simple and as hard as that."

But don't overwork yourself

Do you know the famous line from Stephen King's *The Shining*? "All work and no play makes Jack a dull boy." Just like in the movie, starving yourself of everything but work will only lead to unhappiness.

Using timelines and schedules allows you to more precisely factor how long specific tasks will take, and helps ensure you're not under any undue pressure when it comes to delivering to the client. Of course, the design process usually takes longer than most people think, and a certain level of overwork comes with the territory.

We all get stuck, no matter who we are

"We all get stuck as designers. Don't forget that," said Eric Karjaluoto of Vancouver-based smashLAB. "No matter who you are, the number of accolades you've received, or the past successes you've had, it's still hard. You can look at this a few ways, but I largely take comfort in it."

SinkIt

By smashLAB

Creative director:
Eric Karjaluoto

Designer:
Peter Pimentel

2005

"Becoming a good designer is, in my mind, directly related to one's curiosity and willingness to work," said Karjaluoto. "If you keep asking questions and deliberately practicing your craft, you get better. It's that simple. So when it feels difficult and you want to scream, grab a pencil and a big blank sheet of paper, and just start drawing. With each iteration you're closer."

Start on the right foot, and stay on the right foot

When you've carefully prepared for a project by asking your client plenty of questions, it makes everything run more smoothly. But don't stop this methodical approach once the questions are answered. Attending to and working through each step of the design process will make things much easier for you in the long run. As strange as it might seem, skipping a step only creates more work for you down the road when your client hasn't received the desired result.

Find common ground

"Perhaps one of the biggest killers of motivation in an identity project is client feedback," said designer and author Armin Vit of UnderConsideration. "Specifically, client feedback that challenges in one way or another the solutions we have presented.

"But for the most part, this is where the real challenge of graphic design lies: finding common ground between you and your client in order to solve a visual problem.

"Remember that there are dozens of ways of visually solving any given problem, and most of them are equally valid."

"If the client has reservations about the size or color of something, try another 12 sizes or colors," said Vit. "If the client doesn't like what you showed her, try another dozen options. It doesn't mean you have to show her all of them, but at the very least, do it for yourself. You owe it not just to your client, but to yourself. Explore."

VisionSpring

By Bryony
Gomez-Palacio
and Armin Vit
of Under
Consideration

2008

Deadline looming

"A deadline can be a designer's greatest single source of motivation," said Blair Thomson of UK design studio biz-R.

It's worth adding that your deadlines must be realistic, so always account for unexpected delays. Otherwise, you'll end up placing yourself under undue pressure.

Think laterally

The brain forms routine patterns, in which the more we carry out the same task, the more ingrained and natural the pattern becomes. Before you know it, you're in a rut.

One of my favorite authors is Edward de Bono, regarded by many as a leader in the field of creative thinking. "Creative thinking is a skill," said de Bono. "It's not just a matter of individual talent. It's not just a matter of sitting by the river and playing Baroque music and hoping you get inspired. That's very weak stuff."

Just as you can learn how to speak another language, so too can you learn how to be creative. The aim of thinking laterally is to consider possibilities that are outside your normal train of thought.

How do you do this? I find that sketching each and every idea that pops into my head, and then studying the sketches with the design brief in hand, allows me to produce more sketches that wouldn't have come to mind without such analysis. Turn your design concepts upside down. Look at them from afar. Ask someone to share some thoughts about your sketches. The more creative your ideas, the happier your client becomes, and the more satisfied you will be with the results.

Improve how you communicate

"The single biggest motivation killer for a young designer is the client who wrecks your designs with seemingly pointless changes and unjustified revisions," said Adrian Hanft, creative director at Red Rocket Media Group in Colorado. "While design school has pumped you full of talent and technical knowledge, most people aren't prepared to deal with the heartbreak that comes with the first time a client transforms your masterpiece into manure.

"To stay motivated, you need to look at every encounter with a client as an opportunity to improve the skills they didn't teach you in school: how to communicate with people. As you get better at educating and interacting with your clients, you'll find that fewer and fewer of your designs get ruined and your great ideas aren't being abandoned on the cutting room floor."

Manage your expectations

If you expect clients to be overjoyed with your design work, you'll miss the opportunity to be pleasantly surprised. In fact, you're only leaving yourself open to disappointment. By maintaining modest expectations, constructive criticism from the client can be much easier to handle.

Always design

"Work on a design piece that really inspires you, whether it's a book, magazine, business card, poster, website, anything that gets your juices flowing," said Antonio Carusone of AisleOne. "Always design, even if you have no purpose. It keeps you fresh and motivated."

Follow your bliss

Author and designer Maggie Macnab of Macnab Design offers some fitting advice: "You have to follow your passion in life, regardless of the consequences. For me, that has meant continually developing as a human being throughout the experiences of my life."

SwanSongs

By
Maggie Macnab

2001

"There's a certain integrity with staying true to your soul, and it carries into all avenues of your life," said Macnab. "If something isn't working for you, find out why. Maybe you are in a learning curve and need further development before you can dovetail with it. Maybe it just really isn't a fit and you need to move on. Explore always and discover. If you feel a quickening in your blood, it's the first indication you're on the right path. Read, look, go, be. Most importantly, love the life you are in. You only have one, and only you can have it."

Maddoux Wey Arabian Horse Farm

By
Maggie Macnab

1985

Not everyone is as fortunate

I once read that if you have change in your pocket you're richer than 70 percent of the people on the planet. It's a sobering thought that helps put our "westernized" lives in context. In the grander scheme of things, I'm incredibly fortunate to have grown up in a secure family environment, with a roof over my head and food on the table.

How does this motivate me? I want the same for the children I hope to raise, and by pushing myself to become a better designer, I can attract more rewarding projects (both financially and emotionally), and help secure a stable future.

Never take financial security for granted, and step back once in a while to look at the bigger picture.

That's motivation.

Chapter ten

Your questions answered

I've been authoring design blogs since 2006, and have received more than 20,000 comments on my 500 or so blog posts. Inevitably, many of these comments pose questions about the design process. Important questions, too.

To save you from scouring through my blog archives for answers, and because I've learned a lot in the meantime, I've chosen 15 critical reader questions and updated my answers here, just for you.

Similar looking logos

Q: I've been accused of ripping off someone's logo today, and would appreciate your advice before replying to the accusation. Basically, both of our logos are very similar, but I wouldn't harm my reputation by copying anyone. How would you deal with this?

A: With millions of companies in existence, and with the most iconic logos being simple in appearance, it's almost guaranteed that if you look hard enough, you'll find a similar design to every other. When a trademark lawyer is assessing the strength of a possible case of copyright infringement, what's most important is whether the two logos are used in the same industry or for the same profession. If they're not, the lawyer will likely tell you there isn't a case. If they are, well, lawyers don't come cheap, so do your research into good ones and be prepared to spend.

U.S.-based designer Mike Davidson has this to say about being original: "Tell yourself at every step in the design process that someone has undoubtedly already thought of this, and then ask yourself what you can do to really set it apart."

In design, and particularly where logos are concerned, it's harder to escape the thought that everything has already been done. Whether that's the case or not, you must push yourself to produce ideas that are original to the best of your knowledge, and never settle on an idea you have seen elsewhere.

Rights of use

Q: When you and your client have settled on a finished identity, do you protect it with a copyright so that they must buy stationery, print collateral, and so on from you?

A: Stationery design should be discussed with your client at the beginning of the working relationship. Identity projects are about more than just a logo. They're about a complete visual identity—from business cards and compliment slips to vehicle graphics and billboard design.

If a client approaches you asking for a logo in isolation (i.e., without application on a range of marketing collateral), you should advise her that in order to get the most value from your working relationship and the design, she should take advantage of the expert guidance you provide regarding how best to apply the logo across the gamut of corporate literature, stationery, and advertising.

Bringing a new designer or design studio on board to design the stationery will likely cost your client more, since the new designer will need to do his own research to get up to speed on the company—something you've already done.

However, if at the beginning of the project your client declined the idea of contracting with you for stationery design, chances are that if you executed each step in the design process like the expert that you are, she'll most likely change her mind and ask you to do it anyway.

With that said, clients should receive full ownership of your design. The only right you should preserve is the right to use the work for self-promotion (i.e., in your portfolio).

Online portfolio creation

Q: Do you have any advice for an aspiring designer who wants to create a professional online design portfolio?

A: Broadly speaking, I've found there are five common design
    portfolio mistakes that if avoided will stand you in good
    stead. Here they are:

- **Overuse of Flash.** Many designers see Flash as a tool to
  showcase how creative they are, but in reality, Flash isn't
  always visitor-friendly. There have been many occasions
  when I've been asked to critique a design portfolio, only
  to get hung up on a very slow-moving progress bar
  telling me how little of the site has actually loaded. Your
  portfolio should load as quickly as possible—at least
  within a couple of seconds—because that's all the time
  you have before your visitor gives up and clicks the
  Back button. You might decide to use Flash designs as a
  small accompaniment to a website, but my advice is to
  steer clear altogether and not overcomplicate things.
  The focus of your portfolio should be the work you have
  created for others, and not the latest web design trick
  you've learned.

- **Using thumbnail squares that don't show what the
  project is.** If you've spent even a short period of time
  browsing portfolios, I'm sure you will have seen at least
  one that displays the work using a grid of thumbnails, in
  which only a small section of each design is showing in
  its respective thumbnail. Visitors are somehow supposed
  to guess what else is in the image before clicking through

the rest, assuming they have time to click on every one of the 20 or 30 squares. This is asking your potential clients to play a game of "guess what's behind the door," and believe me, it's a poor game to play. Show visitors what you can do. Show all of each design. You only have seconds to capture their attention.

- **Hiding contact information.** Visitors will view your website for two main reasons: to see the quality of your work, and to hire you for their design needs.

  Regardless which page of your site a visitor is viewing, it should only take one click to get to your contact information. Making this happen is easy: Just place a Contact button in the hot spots on the page where people are most likely to look, such as in the site navigation at the top or left of the page. Providing more than one way to contact you, such as a telephone number, email address, contact form, Skype username, or post office box, is also helpful.

- **Showing images in isolation.** Even well-respected studios make this mistake—showing images with no description. Without giving details about the project goals, you leave it up to your visitors to judge your work on aesthetics alone. But to truly judge how good your design work is, visitors need to know the story behind it: your reasons for choosing a particular design, how it's relevant for the company it identifies, and what image your client wanted to portray. It's these details that can really make your portfolio stand out.

- **Background music.** I'm surprised I need to mention this, but automatically loading background music is one way to have your potential client disappear before you can say, "Come ba... ." Just because there's an option to mute the sound, doesn't mean your client will bother. And who's to say how loud your visitor's speaker volume is? You could have the best music taste in the world, but forcing it on others is a bad idea.

So that's a little about what *not* to do when creating a design portfolio. Now let's talk about what you *should* do.

I began my main blog at davidairey.com back in October 2006. Prior to its launch, and for at least a few months afterward, I had no idea if such an addition to my static portfolio would help me attract new clients. But my website has since grown to become the cornerstone of my business, and, together with my second blog at logodesignlove.com, it receives more than 250,000 visitors per month, with approximately 1 million monthly page views.

You can achieve that, too. In fact, you can surpass it, and your first step—if you haven't already done so—is to launch your blog. Think of it this way: Without me publishing a design blog, you wouldn't be reading this book, because my publisher would never have known to ask me to write it. Put another way, how and what you write about can give potential clients huge insights into your talents and professionalism.

Your articles can also go a long way toward helping you achieve "first page" search-engine rankings. At the time of this writing, if you were to search Google for "graphic designer," you would find me in the top 10 results. I simply could not have achieved that without the work I put into my blog.

If my clients don't find me through an online search, they find me through word of mouth via another client who found me through my online articles. It's an incredible sales tool, and one that also acts as a significant learning tool. The comments my readers leave on individual blog posts have taught me a great deal about design, printing, search engine optimization, marketing, branding, social media, and lots more. To them—to you—I owe a great deal.

One way to set up your own blog is to visit WordPress.org and download the freely available blogging platform. The only costs you incur are the price of a domain name and an annual web hosting package. I use GoDaddy for domain names, and Crucial Web Hosting or ICDSoft for hosting. You may find more suitable providers, but they work well for my purposes.

Seal the deal

Q. Do you have any tips for convincing clients to work with you? I get a lot of inquiries, but very few potential clients go on to hire me.

A. It's always worth reinforcing to clients that the design process is an investment and not simply a cost. Tell them that building brand recognition and brand association are a company's biggest and most valued assets.

In addition, your website should be an invaluable source of help when it comes to clinching a client agreement. You must present yourself in a professional manner. That said, if you have a Facebook account, and you use it for personal photos and chat, keep it for your friends only. Potential clients will check up on your trustworthiness. You can be sure of that.

Speaking of trust, another tip is to show client testimonials on your website. You want people to know what others think about the service you provide, so at the end of every project, be sure to ask for their thoughts. But when asking, don't specifically use the word "testimonial" because it's like trying to put positive thoughts in your clients' mouths. Instead, ask what they thought of the working relationship. Ask what was good and bad about the whole process. That way, not only will you get something positive to add to your website (on a testimonials page, for example), but you will also learn how to improve upon what you do.

I go one step further and ask for a small photo of my client to display alongside the testimonial. This can provide a greater sense of validity to the words you show.

Overseas clients

Q. I've found that a few companies were reluctant to hire me as their designer because I'm in a different country. Does the distance really affect the process?

A. The vast majority of my clients are overseas. This is mainly a result of my strong global search engine rankings, but also, gratefully, due to word of mouth—for instance, I will work with one client in Canada, and she'll tell a business friend of hers about me, leading to another overseas client.

Having a physical location in a different country from many clients hasn't adversely affected any of my design projects. Communicating via telephone, video chat, email, and instant messaging provides ample opportunity for the working relationship to run smoothly.

How many concepts?

Q. How many design concepts should you present to clients?

A. Sometimes one is all it takes, but more often than not, I'll give my clients a choice of two or three. Think about it. If you were having another designer create your brand identity, would you be okay with accepting the one design he gives you, or would you be happier to get a choice?

You're much more likely to reach a smooth agreement when you involve your clients as much as possible.

Be wary of presenting too many concepts, however, because it's a lot easier to choose one from two than it is to choose one from 10—even if all 10 ideas are good.

I see a lot of designers using online client questionnaires in which one of the questions they ask is, "How many concepts do you need?" The question will be followed by a choice of one, two, three, or four. This is bad practice. How can your client determine how many ideas are needed before the right one is created? You, as the designer, can't even answer this question until you have begun designing.

If clients ask how many ideas they will receive, it's much better to say, "between one and four," than to have them choose four, charge them more money, and then force yourself into the possibility of having to present a weak idea. Remember, this isn't a dog and pony show. You're working through a stringent process to determine the strongest results. The number of possibilities can only be determined during the course of the project. Not before.

Friends and family

Q. What are your thoughts about doing design work for close friends and family? How do you work out your prices for them?

I'm always conflicted about this because I know they expect a reduced price, and I don't want to be the bad guy by refusing. They usually don't know the time it takes to complete design work, so in their minds they believe it can be done on the cheap.

A. I'm reluctant to work with friends or family because there's always a danger that exchanging money between people close to you can ruin your relationship.

But, of course, it can also be difficult to say, "No."

You should treat your relations as you would a normal client, and don't neglect the terms and conditions you usually work under. You might feel compelled to offer a discount, but ask yourself if a lower rate is worth a potentially damaged relationship. If you do offer a discount, be sure to show it on your invoice. This will reaffirm to your friend or family member that she is getting a very good deal.

Design revisions

Q. How many revision rounds do you allow your clients?

A. When I started in self-employment, I would always tell clients at the beginning of the project that they could expect *x* number of concepts and *x* number of revision rounds, and that anything else would cost extra. Now that I have more experience, I can see the flaws in that method.

What happens if you tell a client you will create two concepts with two rounds of revisions on a chosen option, but, after which, you know the result is poor? Do you go ahead and supply a poor design because your client hasn't paid you more money? Absolutely not. By specifying a number at the outset, all you're doing is limiting the results. We can't produce iconic designs at every attempt, just like an Olympic runner won't come first in every race. You can determine the amount of necessary designs only during the course of the project.

Project time frames

Q. I'm always asked how long it will take to create a brand identity, but can never seem to give an accurate answer. What do you tell clients?

A. I also find this difficult because projects always differ. There are so many variables, such as how closely involved your client wants to be and how many revisions it takes before both of you are satisfied with the result. You might also arrive at an iconic design within a few hours of sketching, whereas at other times it could take a week of exploration.

During initial discussions, I tell clients that time frames range from two weeks to three months. It's not until you've created a detailed design brief that you can be more specific with your client, and you may well find a project could only take one week, or it might turn into a six-month gig.

The short version is, give your client a range of times, and tell him you can be more specific once you both have signed off on the design brief.

Researching the competition

Q. How much research do you conduct into your client's competitors?

A. A great deal. I mentioned previously in this book that if your client is to win (i.e., gain an edge within his market), then there must be a loser. It might sound a little harsh, but that's business, and you're being paid to increase the profits of your client.

Quantifying the amount of research into an actual figure or timescale isn't possible, because—and I hope you haven't grown tired of me telling you—each project is different, and every client will have a different amount of competition within the particular niche.

Internships

Q: Do you recommend that young designers gain experience through an internship?

A: The value of an internship depends on two things: the quality of the company you're interning with, and your willingness to learn. I interned for three months with the Graphic Arts Technical Foundation in Pittsburgh (now the

Printing Industries of America). I learned a great deal, but that's not to say you can't achieve iconic design without such an internship.

If you're looking for work experience, contact the companies you want to learn from, regardless whether they advertise for interns. The same applies when looking for jobs.

Rather than compete against the hundreds of applicants who search through the same job boards, make a list of respected companies responsible for excellent design work, find out who is responsible for hiring, and send them a handwritten letter introducing yourself and saying you will follow up with a phone call.

Most importantly, be humble. There will always be something to learn about the profession, and especially at this stage in your career. Show that you want to learn.

Worst client project

Q. What has been the worst experience you've had with a client, and what did you learn from it?

A. I generally don't classify any experience as the *worst*, because even when things don't work out as I hope, I learn what *not* to do for the next project. That said, I look back at a number of projects and wonder how I could've improved communication between myself and my clients. There were a couple of times when I had received the client's 50-percent down payment, we'd worked through a number of ideas, but then came a prolonged silence with no response from the client.

To this day, I still have projects that were never finished, and the onus was left on the clients to contact me when they were ready to pick things up again. We're talking about a three-year gap from the last point of communication, and projects in which most of the work was completed. The clients either lost interest or motivation, or their priorities were simply diverted elsewhere.

And therein also lies the importance of receiving a down payment, because otherwise your client might disappear and leave you even further out of pocket.

Tools of the trade

Q. I'm just starting to learn about brand identity, and I'm not entirely sure what hardware and software I should be using. What do you recommend?

A. For hardware, I use a Mac, but you can do exactly the same job with a PC. For software, I use Adobe's Creative Suite, and when developing logos, I stick with Adobe Illustrator.

Some aspiring designers have told me they use Adobe Photoshop to create logos, but you should leave this program for photos. Where logos come into play, you need the design to be scalable to any size (for use on billboards or on the side of buildings, for example), and Illustrator is the industry standard for producing vector artwork. Ultimately, the most important tool you use is your brain. Pencil and paper come a close second.

Handling the workload

Q. As a one-person studio, how do you decide how many clients you take on at any one time?

A. During the design process, there will inevitably be periods when you are awaiting client feedback, so it makes sense to accept more than one project at a time. This way, you can ensure there are no large gaps in your working schedule and that you're not left waiting for what could be days at a time before you continue.

You must be wary, however, of taking on too much work, and I never accept any more than three or four clients at once. This number might differ depending upon the scope of each individual project, and whether you work alone or as part of a studio or agency.

And don't think you need to accept every client that comes your way. Just as a company or organization chooses a designer, you should also choose your clients.

Who owns what?

Q. I spent five years working on brand identity projects within a design agency, and have now decided to set up business on my own. My past employer won't let me use my work in my portfolio. Can he really stop me from doing so?

A. Most employment contracts will stipulate that any work you create during the term of employment belongs to your employer, so you should check to see if it is, indeed, included.

When design agencies subcontract their work to self-employed designers, they will normally want the agreement to remain confidential, and you won't be able to use your designs for future self-promotion. This is why I tell agencies from the outset that should we work together, I retain the right to use all design concepts in my portfolio. It can be frustrating when you produce excellent work, but are then unable to share it with your peers.

If you have a question that hasn't been answered here, then by all means stop by my website at davidairey.com, where I have a comprehensive FAQ section, and where you can contact me directly. I'm a friendly chap.

Chapter eleven

25 practical logo design tips

We've covered a lot of ground up to this point. Although writing about the design process and all its intricacies could amount to at least 10 books of a similar size, let alone one, by now you should have a firm grasp of what's required to go out and create your own iconic brand identities.

This last chapter of the book provides a quick design course for those looking for a brief roundup. Here you will find a rundown of 25 tips, and while many of them have been discussed in more detail in previous chapters, there are a few noted for the first time.

You'll also find additional designs peppered throughout these last pages of our journey together. Hopefully, you'll find them as enjoyable as I do.

1. Questions, questions, questions

From the very beginning of any design project, you need to ask your client questions. Lots of them. You need to have a comprehensive understanding of your client's desires, as well as whom its competitors are, and what's been done with past identities. The last thing you want is to discover near the end of the project that a previously unknown client's competitor uses a similar mark, or that the style of design just simply doesn't relate to your client's goals.

2. Understand print costs

Ask your client very early if she has set a printing budget, because color usually costs more and may limit the scope of your design. Every printer's prices are unique. With some printers, you might find that full-color print costs are nearly on par with single-color jobs, but this is usually rare. It's your job to inform the client about commercial print requirements and limitations early in the process.

Club Collective

By Bunch

2006

club collillective™

3. Expect the unexpected

If you're unsure how long a task will take to complete, always estimate longer. For instance, if you think it will take one week to act upon client feedback and to deliver revised artwork, say it takes two, then pleasantly surprise your client by delivering sooner than expected. Design projects are like construction work—you piece lots of little elements together to form a greater whole, and setbacks can crop up at any time.

4. A logo doesn't need to say what a company does

The Tiger Woods logo isn't a golf club. The Virgin Atlantic logo isn't an airplane. The Xerox logo isn't a photocopier.

Computer logos don't need to show computers, dentist logos don't need to show teeth, and furniture store logos don't need to show furniture.

Just because it's relevant, doesn't mean you can't do better using a design that doesn't depict the product or service your client provides.

5. Not every logo needs a mark

Sometimes your client just needs a professional logotype to identify its business. Use of a symbol can be an unnecessary addition.

This is something you want to determine at the outset of the project. Ask your client if she has a preference one way or another. If the company is entertaining ideas about future expansion into other markets, it might be better to opt for a distinctive logotype, because an identifying mark or symbol might prove restrictive.

6. One thing to remember

All strong logos have one single feature that helps them stand out. Apple's is the bite (or byte). Mercedes is the three-pointed star. The Red Cross is, well, the *red cross*.

Leave your client with just one thing to remember about the brand identity design you've created.

One thing. Not two, three, or four.

Just one.

Ratio

By Fertig Design

2007

RAT/O

7. Don't neglect the sketchpad

You don't need to be an artist to realize the benefits of sketching during the design process. Imaginative ideas flow much faster when you use a pen and paper compared to a mouse and monitor. Carry a notebook with you at all times.

Red66

By Mike Rohde

2006

8. Leave trends to the fashion industry

Trends come and go. When you're talking about changing a pair of jeans, or buying a new dress, then going with the trends can work for you. But where your client's brand identity is concerned, longevity is key.

Don't follow the pack.

Stand out.

City Direct

By Logo Motive Designs

2009

9. Step away from Photoshop

There are a ton of logo design tutorials online that show how to create a logo in Photoshop. Avoid them. We're dealing with vector graphics here, so Adobe Illustrator should be your software of choice. Leave Photoshop for photos.

10. Work in black and white

No amount of fancy gradients or color choices will rescue a poorly designed mark.

By refraining from using color until the end of the process, you and your client are free from distractions of a preference for, say, green, which leaves you free to focus on the idea.

Sacrosanct Roots

By
Michael Kosmicki

2008

11. Keep it relevant

Are you designing for a law firm? Then ditch the fun approach. Perhaps your client produces a kid's TV show. OK, so nothing too serious. Maybe you are designing for a Michelin star restaurant. In this case, you'll likely favor muted colors over bright, fluorescent ones. I could go on, but you get the picture.

12. Remember legibility

The public most likely will glance at the logos you design for only a second or two before moving on. So legibility is key, especially when the brand isn't well-known. For instance, a client's handwriting may look pretty, but if most people can't read it immediately, then don't consider using it as a logotype.

13. Be consistent

Many logos are accompanied by style guides, and the creation of these guides is your responsibility. They ensure that anyone within the client's company who uses the design does so in a consistent manner. Consistency breeds trust. Trust wins customers.

City of Melbourne

By Landor Associates

Creative director:
Jason Little

Designers:
Jason Little,
Sam Pemberton,
Ivana Martinovic,
Jefton Sungkar,
Malin Holmstrom

2009

CITY OF MELBOURNE

14. Match the type to the mark

Display a level of unity across your design. For example, if you show a playful mark, try matching it with a playful typeface.

Ann

By Kevin Burr,
Ocular Ink

2007

ann

15. Offer a single-color version

The logo you design for your client might show a number of different colors, but you must also supply a version that uses just one. By doing so, you'll improve the overall versatility of the identity and save your client from having to come back to you if the company opts for a single-color print run.

16. Pay attention to contrast

When your logo is applied to the design of promotional material or corporate stationery, you must keep an eye on the contrast between the logo and its background, as well as between actual elements within the logo design. The tonal range should be contrasting enough to allow the mark or symbol to be clearly identified.

17. Aid recognition

Keeping your design simple makes it easier for people to recognize it the next time they see it. Consider large corporations like Mitsubishi, Samsung, FedEx, and BBC. Their logos are simple in appearance, and they're easier to recognize because of it. Keeping it simple also allows for flexibility in size. Ideally, your logo will work at a minimum of around one inch without loss of detail.

18. Test at a variety of sizes

Try printing your work to ensure it's clean, with a good level of contrast on paper, and not pixelated. But don't just print a single logo. Replicate the design at a range of sizes and colors for variation. There's no point in using a full page of paper for just one tiny design.

19. Reverse it

Offer clients a logo option that works on dark backgrounds—
in other words, supply a white version. This increases flexibility,
and you'll be appreciated for it.

---

amp

By Fertig Design

2005

amp

20. Turn it upside down

Just because your design looks OK the right way up doesn't
mean it will look OK when viewed upside down. If your logo
appears on a book on a coffee table, for example, you don't
want people who are viewing it upside down to see a phallic
symbol. So consider your design from all angles before
finalizing it.

21. Consider trademarking your design

Having your logo registered as a trademark can prevent legal issues for your client. Unfortunately, the actual registration process is lengthy and complex, so it's worth passing the project to a trademark lawyer. But you should brush up on your knowledge of the process so that you're prepared for questions your lawyer will have for you.

**Channel 4
(rebrand)**

By Rudd Studio

Creative director:
Brett Foraker

2005

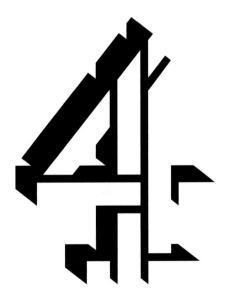

22. Don't neglect the substrate

The paper or card stock on which a logo appears can make a very big difference in how it appears on final presentation. The color and sharpness of your logo can change dramatically. So be sure to discuss all the possibilities for variation with your commercial printer (or advise your client about it) before final production.

23. Don't be afraid of mistakes

Everyone makes mistakes. Learn from them, and move on.

Voodoo

By nido

2007

24. A logo is not a brand

A logo is just one part of a company's brand identity. The brand, as a whole, represents much more—the mission of the company, its history, people's perceptions of it, and so on. An effective logo plays an important part, but it won't save a poor product or service, or a company with a weak mission.

25. Remember, it's a two-way process

Projects do not always pan out the way you think they will. Your client might request something you don't initially agree with. If this happens, work with him on what he wants, and if you still disagree, then show what you believe is an improvement, and give your reasons why. Your clients will be more open to your ideas if you're open to theirs.

Finale

By
Muamer Adilovic

2007

Thanks very much for joining me on this brief journey through the design process. For up-to-date logo news and reviews, head over to the online presence of Logo Design Love: www.logodesignlove.com.

Help from elsewhere

Graphic design blogs

Logo Design Love	logodesignlove.com
David Airey	davidairey.com
Ace Jet 170	acejet170.com
AisleOne	aisleone.net
Brand New	underconsideration.com/brandnew
Coudal Partners	coudal.com
Creative Review Blog	creativereview.co.uk/crblog
davidthedesigner	davidthedesigner.com
Design Notes	designnotes.info
Design Observer	designobserver.com
Design View	andyrutledge.com
Dexigner	dexigner.com
FormFiftyFive	formfiftyfive.com
grain edit	grainedit.com
ideasonideas	ideasonideas.com
Identity Forum	identityworks.com/forum
I Love Typography	ilovetypography.com
thought for the week	johnsonbanks.co.uk/thoughtfortheweek
Noisy Decent Graphics	noisydecentgraphics.typepad.com
SeptemberIndustry	septemberindustry.co.uk
Subtraction	subtraction.com
swissmiss	swiss-miss.com
Swiss Legacy	swisslegacy.com
The Dieline	thedieline.com
The Grid System	thegridsystem.org
Veer	blog.veer.com

Iconic designers

Otl Aicher
Saul Bass
Michael Bierut
Robert Brownjohn
Ken Cato
Ivan Chermayeff
Joe Finocchiaro
Alan Fletcher
Tom Geismar
Steff Geissbuhler
Milton Glaser
Gene Grossman
Sagi Haviv
Armin Hofmann
Gerard Huerta
Michael Johnson
Yusaka Kamekura
Jerry Kuyper

Lindon Leader
Raymond Loewy
Herb Lubalin
Marcello Minale
Per Mollerup
Morteza Momayez
Miles Newlyn
Paul Rand
Paula Scher
Sven Seger
Anton Stankowski
Henry Steiner
Brian Tattersfield
Roger van den Bergh
Massimo Vignelli
Bob Wolf
Michael Wolff
Lance Wyman

Biographical info and web addresses for these designers can be found on the iconic logo designer website: logosdesigners.com

Recommended books

Identity design process

Designing Brand Identity: An Essential Guide for the Whole Branding Team
By Alina Wheeler

Logo Savvy: Top Brand Design Firms Share their Naming and Identity Strategies
By Perry Chua, Dann Ilicic

Decoding Design: Understanding and Using Symbols in Visual Communication
By Maggie Macnab

Before the Brand: Creating the Unique DNA of an Enduring Brand Identity
By Alycia Perry

Thinking

Cradle to Cradle: Remaking the Way We Make Things
By William McDonough, Michael Braungart

A Technique for Producing Ideas (Advertising Age Classics Library)
By James Young

Lateral Thinking: Creativity Step by Step (Perennial Library)
By Edward De Bono

Change the Way You See Everything Through Asset-Based Thinking
By Kathryn D. Cramer, Hank Wasiak

It's Not How Good You Are, It's How Good You Want to Be: The World's Best Selling Book
By Paul Arden

Whatever You Think, Think the Opposite
by Paul Arden

Graphic design

How To Be a Graphic Designer Without Losing Your Soul
By Adrian Shaughnessy

79 Short Essays on Design
By Michael Bierut

Graphic Design as a Second Language: Bob Gill (Hands on Graphics)
By Bob Gill

Studio Culture: The Secret Life of a Graphic Design Studio
By Adrian Shaughnessy, Tony Brook

Graphic Design, Referenced: A Visual Guide to the Language, Applications, and History of Graphic Design
By Armin Vit, Bryony Gomez Palacio

How to Think Like a Great Graphic Designer
By Debbie Millman

Branding

The Brand Gap: Expanded Edition
By Marty Neumeier

The Truth About Creating Brands People Love
By Brian D. Till, Donna Heckler

Brand Apart
By Joe Duffy

Kellogg on Branding: The Marketing Faculty of The Kellogg School of Management
By Tim Calkins, Alice Tybout

Zag: The Number One Strategy of High-Performance Brands
By Marty Neumeier

Trust Agents: Using the Web to Build Influence, Improve Reputation, and Earn Trust
By Chris Brogan, Julien Smith

Typography

Stop Stealing Sheep & Find Out How Type Works (2nd Edition)
By Erik Spiekermann, E.M Ginger

Thinking with Type: A Critical Guide for Designers, Writers, Editors, & Students (Design Briefs)
By Ellen Lupton

The New Typography (Weimar and Now: German Cultural Criticism)
By Jan Tschichold

The Elements of Typographic Style
By Robert Bringhurst

Logo, Font & Lettering Bible
By Leslie Cabarga

Designing with Type: The Essential Guide to Typography
By James Craig, William Bevington, Irene Korol Scala

Iconic designers

Paul Rand: Modernist Designer
By Derek Birdsall, Steven Heller, Nathan Garland, Paul Rand, Milton Glaser, Ivan Chermayeff

Milton Glaser: Graphic Design
By Milton Glaser

Six Chapters in Design: Saul Bass, Ivan Chermayeff, Milton Glaser, Paul Rand, Ikko Tanaka, Henryk Tomaszewski
By Philip Meggs

Lella and Massimo Vignelli (International Graphic Design)
By Images Publishing Group

Paul Rand
By Steven Heller

Index
Looking for something?

A

Ace Jet 170 design blog, 147
adaptability, 34–35
additional service and support, 78–79
Adilovic, Muamer, 191
Adobe Creative Suite, 175
Adobe Illustrator, 175–176, 183
Adobe Photoshop, 114–116, 176
Airey, David
    Berthier Associates brand identity project by, 120–122, 136–138
    Circle sketches by, 110
    Ecometrica mind map by, 94
    Ecometrica sketches by, 96
    Komplett Fitness mind map by, 91
    Meadows Renewable mind map by, 92
    Originn and Henri Ehrhart logos by, 150
    Yellow Pages logo redesign by, 139–140
AisleOne, 157
Amanda Marsden logotype, 18–20
amp logo, 188
Ann logo, 186
answers. see questions answered
anxiety
    at presentations, 118
    at project onset, 42–43
Arnell Group, 63–65
Arnell, Peter, 63–65
art of conversation
    avoiding intermediation, 126–128
    conspiring with point of contact, 124–125
    dealing with decision-making committees, 119–123
    keeping the committee involved, 132–134
    overview, 118–119
    swallowing your pride, 136–141
    taking control, 128–131
    under-promising and over-delivering, 134–136
audience, 46–47
Awards for National Newspaper Advertising (ANNAs) logo, 31

B

background music, 165
balance, 150
Bartow, Doug, 11
Berthier Associates brand identity project

    dealing with decision-maker and, 120–122
    swallowing pride and, 136–138
Berthier, Dominique, 120–122
biz-R design studio
    Amanda Marsden logotype by, 18–20
    Blair Thomson of, 154
    Clive's brand identity by, 50–52
black and white
    before color, 111–113, 184
    for distinction, 30–31
Brain Longevity (Khalsa), 2
brand identity. see also identity
    for Berthier Associates, 120–122
    for Clive's, 50–52
    for Federal Express Corporation, 53–56
    for Harned, Bachert & Denton, LLP, 59–61
    for Heart Hospital of New Mexico, 56–58
    importance of, 8, 21
    logos as part of, 190
    need for new, 46–47
    redesigning. see redesign
Bunch
    Club Collective logo by, 179
    The Star of Bethnal Green logo by, 13–17
Burr, Kevin, 186

C

Carusone, Antonio, 157
Channel 4 logo, 189
Chermayeff & Geismar, 145, 146
Chermayeff, Ivan
    HarperCollins logo by, 146
    Showtime logo by, 145
CIGNA Corporation, redesign, 69–72
Circle sketches, 110
City Direct logo, 183
City of Melbourne logo, 185
client(s)
    common ground with, 153–154
    competition, researching, 173
    friends as, 170–171
    giving time and space to, 48
    initial anxiety of, 42–43
    needs, bringing to life, 56–58
    overseas, 168–169
    questions for, 44–47
    testimonials, 167–168

worst projects of, 174–175
Clive's brand identity, 50–52
Club Collective logo, 179
Coca-Cola redesign, 66–68
color
    vs. black and white, 30, 111–113, 184
    print costs and, 179
    single, 186
    W.K. Kellogg and, 9
committee, decision-making
    avoiding design by, 123
    dealing with, 119–123
    staying involved, 132–134
common ground, 153–154
communication skills, 156. see also art of conversation
computers
    sketchpads and, 96–97
    stepping away from, 149
concepts
    how many to present, 169–170
    mind-mapping and. see mind maps
    Photoshop and, 114–116
    presenting. see art of conversation
consistency, 185
contact information, 164
contrast
    for distinction, 30–32
    paying attention to, 187
control, 128–131
conversation. see art of conversation
copyright, 160–162
costs. see print costs
Creative Curio, 150
Creative Suite (Adobe), 175
creative thinking, 155. see also mind maps
criteria, project, 56–58
Crucial Web Hosting, 167

D

Daily Nest mind map, 95
davidairey.com, 165, 177
Davidson Locksmith logo, 124–125
Davidson, Mike, 161
Davidson, Paul, 124–125
davidthedesigner.com, 147
de Bono, Edward, 155
deadlines
    keeping to, 134–136
    motivation and, 154
decision-maker. see committee, decision-making
demand level, 79
design blog(s)
    Ace Jet 170, 145–146
    Creative Curio, 150
    Logo Design Love, 165, 191
    questions and answers. see questions answered
    setting up, 166–167
design brief
    assembling, 49–50
    for Clive's, 50–52

role of, 43–44
design by committee, 123
design courses, 88
design inspiration. see motivation
design ownership, 177
design portfolios. see online design portfolios
design presentations. see art of conversation
design pricing formula
    additional service and support, 78–79
    current economy, 80
    demand level, 79
    level of expertise, 77
    overview, 76–77
    project specifications/turnaround time, 78
design revisions, 171–172
desire, and motivation, 151
distinction, 30–31
down payments, 84–85

E

Earnheart + Friends of Bowling Green, Kentucky, 60
Ecometrica, 93–94, 96
economic situation, 80, 159
Ed's Electric logo, 26
Elemental8 logo, 107–109
endurance, 28–29
Enns, Blair, 123, 124, 128, 131
exchange rates, 85–86
expectations, 156
expertise, 77

F

Federal Express Corporation (FedEx)
    field research for, 53–56
    logo by Lindon Leader, 23
feedback, 136–141
Fertig Design
    amp logo by, 188
    Ratio logo by, 181
field research
    of companies and products, 48–49
    for Federal Express Corporation, 53–56
    for Heart Hospital of New Mexico, 57
Filmaps.com logo, 102–103
Finale logo, 191
financial security, 159
Flash designs, 163
flexibility, 188
focus
    groups, redesign and, 68–69
    maintaining, 48
    single, 36–37, 139
Foraker, Brett, 189
forums, online design, 88
French Property Exhibition logo, 36–37
Fresh Machine, 8
friends, as clients, 170–171
Fusion logo, 148

G

Geismar, Tom, 145
genuine product, 9
GoDaddy domain name search tool, 167
Gomez-Palacio, Bryony, 154
Graphic Arts Technical Foundation, 173
Grear, Malcolm
    New Bedford Whaling Museum logo by, 32–33
    Vanderbilt University logo by, 28–29
ground rules
    beginning, 133–134
    at committee meetings, 129–130
    reminders about, 136
groundwork, for iconic design
    asking questions, 45–47
    assembling design brief, 49–50
    gathering information, 44–45
    giving client time and space, 48
    overview, 42
    reviewing information/researching company, 48–49
    role of design brief, 43–44
    shaking out jitters, 42–43
Guild of Food Writers logo, 7

H

Hanft, Adrian, 156
hardware, for identity design, 175–176
Harned, Bachert & Denton (HBD) logo, 59–61
HarperCollins logo, 146
Harry Potter and the Deathly Hallows (Rowling), 11
Hawaiian Airlines logo, 25
Heart Hospital of New Mexico redesign, 56–58
Helvetica Neue typeface, 73–75
Henri Ehrhart logo, 150
Holmstrom, Malin, 185
hourly rates vs. set fee, 81–82
HOWDesign.com, 88
Huerta, Gerard, 10
Hyde, David, 147

I

ICDSoft web hosting, 167
iconic design, elements
    adaptable, 34–35
    distinctive, 30–31
    enduring, 28–29
    memorable, 32–33
    overview, 22
    relevant, 25–27
    simple, 22–24
    single focus, 36–37
    summary, 38–39
iconic design, groundwork. *see* groundwork, for iconic design
id29 design studio, 11
identity. *see also* brand identity
    for Clive's, 50–52
    for Federal Express Corporation, 53–56
    for Harned, Bachert & Denton, LLP, 59–61
    for Heart Hospital of New Mexico, 56–58
    importance of, 21
    language-centric approach to, 18–20
    logos and, 10
    redesigning. *see* redesign
Illustrator (Adobe), 175–176, 183
images, in isolation, 164–165
information gathering
    bringing to life, 56–58
    preliminary, 44–45
    tougher questions for, 45–47
inspiration. *see* motivation
intermediation, 126–128
internships, 173–174

J

JCJ Architecture logotype, 72–75
Jerry Kuyper Partners, 148
Jost, Josiah
    Ed's Electric logo by, 26
    Filmaps.com logo by, 102–103

K

Karjaluoto, Eric, 152
Kellogg, Will Keith, 9
Kellogg's Corn Flakes, 9
Kerling logo mockups, 114–116
Khalsa, Dharma Singh, 2
Komplett Fitness
    logo, 135–136
    mind map, 91
Kosmicki, Michael, 184
Kovac, Denis, 13–15
Krause, Lauren, 150
Kuyper, Jerry, 148

L

La Internacional logo, sketching examples, 104–106
Landor Associates
    City of Melbourne logo by, 185
    Federal Express Corporation and, 54–56
language-centric approach, 18–20
lateral thinking, 155
Law, David, 30–31
Lawless, Martin, 151
laying the groundwork. *see* groundwork, for iconic design
Leader Creative design firm, 69–72
learning, 145–147
legibility, in iconic design, 185
level of demand, 79
level of expertise, 77
Lexus logo, 7
Lindon Leader
    FedEx design by, 23, 55
    Hawaiian Airlines logo by, 25
listening skills, 136–141

Little, Jason, 185
LodgeNet logo, 148
logo design contests, 87–88
logo design tips
    asking questions, 178
    avoiding trends/Photoshop, 183
    dealing with substrates, mistakes and
    brand identity, 190
    expecting the unexpected, 179
    importance of sketchpads, 182
    maintaining legibility and consistency, 185
    matching type to mark/single color
    version, 186
    no identifying mark/symbol, 180
    not depicting the product/service, 180
    noting contrast/simplicity/testing sizes, 187
    registration as trademark, 189
    relevance, 184
    reversing and turning upside down, 188
    two-way process, 191
    understanding print costs, 179
    working in black and white, 184
logodesignlove.com, 165, 191
logos. *see also* iconic design, elements
    bombardment of, 2–7
    rights of use, 161–162
    similar looking, 160–161
    style guide for, 47
longevity, in iconic design, 28–29

M

Macnab Design, 157
Macnab, Maggie
    Heart Hospital of New Mexico and, 56–58
    SwanSongs logo by, 157–158
    Maddoux Way Arabian Horse Farm logo, 158
Malcolm Grear Designers
    New Bedford Whaling Museum logo by, 32–33
    Vanderbilt University logo by, 28–29
Martinez, Julio
    Elemental8 logo by, 107–109
    La Internacional logo by, 104–106
Martinovic, Ivana, 185
Meadows Renewable mind map, 92
memorable design, 32–33
mind maps
    Daily Nest, 95
    Ecometrica, 93–94
    Komplett Fitness, 91
    Meadows Renewable, 92
    overview, 90–91
mistakes
    in design portfolios. *see* online design portfolios
    learn from, 190
    in setting prices, 89
mockups, in Photoshop, 114–116
Molly Designs, 8
monogram, for Woodmere Art Museum, 111–113
Moon Brand
    National Health Service logo by, 24

    The Royal Parks logo by, 12
    Vision Capital logo by, 27
Moon, Richard, 12, 24, 27
Morgan, Katie, 7
motivation
    actively learning, 145–147
    always designing, 157
    balancing your life, 150
    creating for yourself, 148
    financial security as, 159
    finding common ground, 153–154
    following your passion, 157–158
    getting stuck and, 152
    improving communication/managing expectations, 156
    looking back in time, 150
    looming deadlines as, 154
    overview, 144
    showing relentless desire/not overworking, 151
    starting on the right foot, 153
    staying four years ahead, 147
    stepping away from computers, 149
    thinking laterally for, 154

N

National Health Service (NHS) logo, 24
New Bedford Whaling Museum logo, 32–33
new Coke, rebranding, 66–68
Newspaper Marketing Agency (NMA) logos, 30–31
nido design and visual communications
    Talkmore logo by, 31
    Voodoo logo by, 190
nonprofit organizations, 88

O

Ocular Ink graphic design studio, 186
Ogden, Stephen Lee, 59–61
160over90 design agency, 111–113
online design forums, 88
online design portfolios
    background music, 165
    contact information hidden, 164
    Flash overuse, 163
    images shown in isolation, 164–165
    launching, 166–167
    thumbnail squares in, 163–164
open mind, 136–141
Originn logo, 150
overseas clients, 168–169
overwork, 151

P

Pantone swatches, 113
passion, 157–158
PDFs (Portable Document Formats). *see* presentation PDFs
Pemberton, Sam, 185
pencil design work to PDFs

mind-mapping. *see* mind maps
overview, 90
presenting PDFs. *see* presentation PDFs
sketching. *see* sketchpad work
summary, 116–117
PepsiCo, 63–65
perspective concept, Woodmere's, 111–112
Photoshop
    presentation PDFs and, 114–116
    stepping away from, 183
Pimentel, Peter, 152
point of contact
    conspiring with, 124–125
    Dominique Berthier as, 120–122
portfolios. *see* online design portfolios
practical tips. *see* logo design tips
presentation PDFs. *see also* pencil design work to PDFs
    best ideas as, 109–110
    black and white before color, 111–113
    using Photoshop, 114–116
presentations. *see* art of conversation
pricing design
    down payments and, 84–85
    exchange rates and, 85–86
    formula. *see* design pricing formula
    handling print costs, 82–84
    hourly rates or set fee, 81–82
    mistakes, 89
    overview, 76
    spec work and, 87–88
pride, 136–141
print costs
    pricing design and, 82–84
    understanding, 179
Printing Industries of America, 174
pro bono design work, 88
project criteria, 56–58
project specifications, 78
project time frames, 172

Q

questions
    for the client, 178
    information gathering and, 45–47
questions answered
    competition research, 173
    design ownership, 177
    design portfolio mistakes. *see* online design portfolios
    design revisions, 171–172
    friends and family, 170–171
    handling the workload, 176–177
    internships, 173–174
    number of concepts, 169–170
    overseas clients, 168–169
    project time frames, 172
    rights of use, 161–162
    sealing the deal, 167–168
    similar looking logos, 160–161
    tools of the trade, 175–176
    worst client projects, 174–175

R

Rand, Paul, 145
Ratio logo, 181
rebranding. *see* redesign
receipt of down payment, 84–86
Red Rocket Media Group, 156
Red66 logo, 182
redesign
    CIGNA Corporation's successful, 69–72
    Coca-Cola's unsuccessful, 66–68
    examining reasons for, 63
    focus groups and, 68–69
    for Heart Hospital of New Mexico, 56–58
    maintaining manners and, 75
    overview, 62
    vs. refinement, 72–75
    Tropicana's unsuccessful, 63–65
    Woodmere Art Museum's successful, 111–113
refinement, 72–75
registration process, 189
relevance, in iconic design, 25–27, 184
research
    of companies and products, 48–49
    for Federal Express Corporation, 53–56
    for Heart Hospital of New Mexico, 57
Rethink Communications, 34–35
Reuters, 7
reversal, 188
revisions, 171–172
Rhode, Mike, 182
Roy Smith design, 36–37
The Royal Parks logo, 12
Rudd Studio, 189
rules, 39. *see also* ground rules
rush job markups, 78

S

Sabatier, Andrew, 114–116
Sacrosanct Roots logo, 184
Scher, Paula, 81, 145
Scion logo, 7
Selikoff + Company, 84
Selikoff, Jonathan, 84–85
service, additional, 78–79
set fees vs. hourly rates, 81–82
Showtime logo, 145
Siah Design
    Ed's Electric logo by, 26
    Filmaps.com logo by, 102–103
signature, trademark
    Kellogg's, 9
    Woodmere's, 111–112
simplicity, in iconic design, 22–24, 34–35, 187
single color, 186
single feature, 181
single focus, 36–37, 139. *see also* focus
SinkIt logo, 152
size, in iconic design, 187
sketchpad work
    Ecometrica examples, 96

Filmaps.com example, 102–103
La Internacional examples, 104–106
necessity of, 96–97, 182
presenting best as PDFs, 109–110
Tenth Avenue Alliance Church examples, 98–101
time frames and, 107–109
smashLAB, 152
Smith, Roy, 36–37
social identification
    importance of, 21
    language-centric approach to, 18–20
    logos and, 10
software, for identity design, 175–176
SomeOne, 30–31
spec work, 87–88
specifications, project, 78
The Star of Bethnal Green (SoBG) logo, 13–17
Star, Rob, 13–14
starting on the right foot, 153
staying motivated. see motivation
story telling, with logos, 8
strategy, 130, 134
studio hyde, 147
studio1500
    Elemental8 logo by, 107–109
    La Internacional logo by, 104–106
style guide, 47
substrates, 190
Sugoi logo, 34–35
Sungkar, Jefton, 185
support, additional, 78–79
swallowing one's pride, 136–141
SwanSongs logo, 157
symbol(s)
    matching typeface to, 186
    transcending boundaries, 13–14
    unnecessary, 180

T

taking control, 128–131
Talkmore logo, 31
Tenth Avenue Alliance Church logos, 98–101
testimonials, 167–168
Thomson, Blair, 154
300million
    The Guild of Food Writers logo by, 7
    Martin Lawless and, 151
thumbnail squares, in design portfolios, 163–164
time
    journeying back in, 150
    sketchpad work and, 107–109
time and space, 48
time frames, 172, 179
TIME logo, 10
tips. see logo design tips
trademark lawyer, 189
trademark signature, 9
trademark signatures, 111–112
tradition, 28–29
trends vs. longevity, 183

Tropicana Pure Premium redesign, 63–65
turnaround time, 78
Type Directors Club logo, 10
typeface, 73–75, 186

U

under-promising and over-delivering service, 134–136
UnderConsideration, 72–75, 153–154
upside down viewpoint, 188

V

Vanderbilt University logo, 28–29
Vision Capital logo, 27
VisionSpring logo, 154
Vit, Armin, 72–75, 153–154
Voodoo logo, 190

W

Waldenbooks logo, 10
web hosting, 167
Weston, Richard, 145–146
Win Without Pitching consulting firm, 123
Woodmere Art Museum rebranding, 111–113
word association, 47, 59–61
WordPress.org, 166–167
workload, 176–177
Wu, Nancy, 34–35, 98–101

Y

Yellow Pages logo redesign, 139–140

Z

Zia sun symbol, 57–58